1938–2011

ROBERT E. COURTEMANCHE

This Winter issue of *Ploughshares* is dedicated to Robert E. Courtemanche, whose generosity and friendship to the magazine have been invaluable over the years.

PLOUGHSHARES
is pleased to announce the winner of its first

EMERGING FICTION WRITER'S CONTEST

SINCE 1971, PLOUGHSHARES has been committed to promoting the work of up-and-coming writers. In the spirit of the magazine's founding mission, the *Ploughshares* Emerging Fiction Writer's Contest recognizes work by an author just beginning to publish.

THIS YEAR'S AWARD:

▸*Winner*: Thomas Lee for "The Gospel of Blackbird." The story can be found on page 123 of this issue, with a profile of the author in the Postscripts section on page 159.

▸*Runner-Up*: Rebecca Leece for "You're So Normal I Could Scream"

▸*Honorable Mentions*: Maria Robinson for "A Gap in the Flashing," and David Meischen for "The Stillness that Waits"

This year's contest was judged by *Ploughshares* co-founder DeWitt Henry.

pshares.org/emergingaward
FOR COMPLETE DETAILS

SUBMISSION POLICIES:

Beginning in 2012, the Emerging Writer's Contest will have separate awards for fiction, nonfiction, and poetry, with a $1,000 prize in each genre.

▸Login to our online submission manager between February 1 and April 2 to submit in one of the genres.

▸The contest rules and a link to the online submission manager, can be found at: pshares.org/emergingaward

▸Please submit only 3–5 poems; nonfiction and fiction entries should be under 5,000 words.

▸The entry fee of $20, payable by credit card on the submission manager site, includes a 1-year subscription to *Ploughshares*. Current subscribers may add to their subscription or give the subscription as a gift.

ELIGIBILITY:
We define an emerging writer as someone who has yet to publish a book and has won no major awards.

PLOUGHSHARES

Winter 2011-12 • Vol. 37, No. 4

GUEST EDITOR
Alice Hoffman

EDITOR-IN-CHIEF
Ladette Randolph

MANAGING EDITOR
Andrea Martucci

FICTION EDITOR
Margot Livesey

POETRY EDITOR
John Skoyles

FOUNDING EDITOR
DeWitt Henry

FOUNDING PUBLISHER
Peter O'Malley

PRODUCTION MANAGER
Akshay Ahuja

EDITORIAL ASSISTANTS
Sarah Banse & Abby Travis

SENIOR READERS
David Goldstein, Linwood Rumney & Abby Travis

INTERNS
Jessica Arnold, Susanna Kellogg & Jordan Koluch

COPY EDITOR
Carol Farash

ePUBLISHING CONSULTANT
John Rodzvilla

READERS

Chandra Asar | Jana Lee Balish | Rowan E. Beaird | Mary Kovaleski Byrnes
Doug Paul Case | Anne Champion | Elizabeth Christensen | Susannah Clark
Joseph Croscup | Lindsay D'Andrea | Ricky Davis | Nicole DiCello | Aiden
FitzGerald | Fabienne Francois | Joshua Gartska | Taylor Gibbs | Kristine Greive
Daniel Gullet | Anna Hofvander | Ethan Joella | Max Kaisler | Jocelyn Kerr | Eson
Kim | Rachel Ko | Aaron Kroll | Andrew Ladd | Jason Lapeze | Karen Lonzo
Sean Mackey | Valerie Maloof | LuzJennifer Martinez | Jean Mattes | Autumn
McClintock | Leslie McIntyre | Danielle Monroe | Eileen Mullan | Katie Murphy
Casey Nobile | Chantal Notarstefano | Kathleen Perruzzi | June Rockefeller
M. Austen Roe | Wesley Rothman | Lindsay Sainlar | Nick Sansone | Ellen
Scheuermann | Mallory Schwan | Charlotte Seley | Ian Singleton | Brooks Sterritt
Sarah Stetson | Katherine Sticca | Sebastian Stockman | Kristen Sund | Jessica
Survelas | Regina Tavani | Gina Tomaine | Angela Voras-Hills | Nico Vreeland
Shannon Wagner | Caitlin Walls | Leah Welch | Caitlin White

ADVISORY BOARD
William H. Berman | DeWitt Henry | Alice Hoffman
Pam Painter | Janet Silver | Daniel Tobin | Marilyn Zacharis

Ploughshares, a journal of new writing, is guest-edited serially by prominent writers who explore different and personal visions, aesthetics, and literary circles. *Ploughshares* is published in April, August, and December at Emerson College, 120 Boylston Street, Boston, MA 02116-4624. Telephone: (617) 824-3757. Web address: pshares.org. E-mail: pshares@emerson.edu.

Advisory Editors: Sherman Alexie, Russell Banks, Andrea Barrett, Charles Baxter, Ann Beattie, Madison Smartt Bell, Anne Bernays, Frank Bidart, Amy Bloom, Robert Boswell, Henry Bromell, Rosellen Brown, Ron Carlson, James Carroll, David Daniel, Madeline DeFrees, Mark Doty, Rita Dove, Stuart Dybek, Cornelius Eady, Martín Espada, B. H. Fairchild, Carolyn Forché, Richard Ford, George Garrett, Lorrie Goldensohn, Mary Gordon, Jorie Graham, David Gullette, Marilyn Hacker, Donald Hall, Joy Harjo, Kathryn Harrison, Stratis Haviaras, Terrance Hayes, DeWitt Henry, Edward Hirsch, Jane Hirshfield, Tony Hoagland, Alice Hoffman, Fanny Howe, Marie Howe, Gish Jen, Justin Kaplan, Bill Knott, Yusef Komunyakaa, Maxine Kumin, Don Lee, Philip Levine, Margot Livesey, Thomas Lux, Gail Mazur, Campbell McGrath, Heather McHugh, James Alan McPherson, Sue Miller, Lorrie Moore, Paul Muldoon, Antonya Nelson, Jay Neugeboren, Howard Norman, Tim O'Brien, Joyce Peseroff, Carl Phillips, Jayne Anne Phillips, Robert Pinsky, Alberto Ríos, Lloyd Schwartz, Jim Shepard, Jane Shore, Charles Simic, Gary Soto, Elizabeth Spires, David St. John, Maura Stanton, Gerald Stern, Mark Strand, Elizabeth Strout, Christopher Tilghman, Richard Tillinghast, Colm Tóibín, Chase Twichell, Jean Valentine, Fred Viebahn, Ellen Bryant Voigt, Dan Wakefield, Derek Walcott, Rosanna Warren, Alan Williamson, Eleanor Wilner, Tobias Wolff, C. D. Wright, Al Young, Kevin Young

Subscriptions (ISSN 0048-4474): $30 for one year (3 issues); $50 for two years (6 issues); $39 a year for institutions. Add $24 a year for international ($10 for Canada).

Upcoming: Spring 2012, a poetry and prose issue edited by Nick Flynn, will be published in April 2012. Fall 2012, a nonfiction issue edited by Patricia Hampl, will be published in August 2012.

Submissions: Ploughshares has an updated reading period, as of June 1, 2010. The new reading period is from June 1 to January 15 (postmark and online dates). All submissions sent from January 16 to May 31 will be returned unread. Please see page 200 for editorial and submission policies, or visit our Web site: pshares.org/submit.

Back-issue, classroom-adoption, and bulk orders may be placed directly through *Ploughshares*. Microfilms of back issues may be obtained from University Microfilms. *Ploughshares* is also available as CD-ROM and full-text products from EBSCO, H. W. Wilson, JSTOR, ProQuest, and the Gale Group. Indexed in M.L.A. Bibliography, Humanities International Index, Book Review Index. Full publishers' index is online at pshares.org. The views and opinions expressed in this journal are solely those of the authors. All rights for individual works revert to the authors upon publication. *Ploughshares* receives support from the National Endowment for the Arts and the Massachusetts Cultural Council.

Retail distribution by Ingram Periodicals, Source Interlink, and Ubiquity. Printed in the U.S.A. by The Sheridan Press.

Alice Hoffman photo by Deborah Feingold.

© 2011 by Emerson College   ISBN 978-1-933058-21-4
ISSN 0048-4474

CONTENTS

Winter 2011-12

INTRODUCTION
Alice Hoffman   6

FICTION
Ruth Blank, *Tomato Season*   11
James Franco, *The Deer*   22
William Giraldi, *Hold the Dark*   36
Jennifer Haigh, *Paramour*   54
Ann Hood, *Code Blue*   66
Joshua Howes, *Run*   75
Rachel Kadish, *The Governess and the Tree*   83
Wally Lamb, *Girl Skipping Rope*   98
Ann Leary, *Safety*   108
Emerging Writer's Contest Winner, selected by DeWitt Henry
    Thomas Lee, *The Gospel of Blackbird*   123

NONFICTION
Bonnie Friedman, *Coming of Age in Book Country*   28

POETRY
Paula Bohince, *Everywhere I Went That Spring, I Was Alone*   9
Martha Collins, *In White*   18
    That Night, I   19
Kerry James Evans, *Blackbird*   20
Ursula K. Le Guin, *Hour of the Changes*   34
    Lorca's Duende   35
Sydney Lea, *Not Like Adamo*   51
Anna Margolin (translated by Maia Evrona), *The Years*   53
J. D. McClatchy, *Prelude, Delay, and Epitaph*   64
Campbell McGrath, *An Irish Word*   78
    The Fly   81
Jennifer Militello, *Antidote with Placebo*   91
Joseph Millar, *Late December*   93

- Marge Piercy, *The night has a long hairy pelt* — 94
  - *The romantic getaway* — 96
  - *Baggage* — 97
- Nicholas Samaras, *I Like to Live with Hermits* — 107

Philip Schultz, *Hitting and Getting Hit* — 119
Megan Sexton, *Ode to Silence* — 122
Sue Standing, *Diamond Haiku* — 137
   Orchard House — 138
   Self-Portrait — 139
Jane Summer, *My Opera Glasses* — 140
Mary Szybist, *Here, There Are Blueberries* — 141
Matthew Thorburn, *"A Field of Dry Grass"* — 142

ABOUT ALICE HOFFMAN — 145
   A Profile by Alexandra Marshall
MESSING ABOUT IN BOATS — 151
   A Plan B Essay by Michael Anania
POSTSCRIPTS — 156
FROM THE ARCHIVE — 161
   George Starbuck, *"The Work!"* : A Conversation with Elizabeth Bishop (Reprinted from Issue 11 of *Ploughshares*, Spring 1977)
BOOKSHELF — 185
   DeWitt Henry reviews *What Is Left the Daughter: A Novel*, by Howard Norman
   Ewa Hryniewicz-Yarbrough reviews *Unseen Hand: Poems*, by Adam Zagajewski
   Jocelyn Lieu reviews *Train Dreams: A Novella*, by Denis Johnson
   Maryanne O'Hara reviews *The Foremost Good Fortune: A Memoir*, by Susan Conley
   Linwood Rumney reviews *How Like Foreign Objects: Poems*, by Alexis Orgera
EDITORS' SHELF — 195
EDITORS' CORNER — 196
CONTRIBUTORS' NOTES — 196

Cover: Barbara Takenaga, *Dione*, 2010, acrylic on canvas, 42" x 36". Courtesy of the Gregory Lind Gallery, San Francisco.

PLOUGHSHARES PATRONS

This nonprofit publication would not be possible without the support of our readers and the generosity of the following individuals and organizations.

CO-PUBLISHERS
Robert E. Courtemanche
The Green Angel Foundation

COUNCIL
Jacqueline Liebergott
Marillyn Zacharis

PATRONS
Eugenia Gladstone Vogel
Denice and Mel Cohen
Thomas E. Martin and Alice S. Hoffman
Dr. Jay A. Jackson and Dr. Mary Anne Jackson
Joanne Randall

FRIENDS
Christopher J. Palermo
William H. Berman
Elizabeth R. Rea of the Dungannon Foundation

ORGANIZATIONS
Emerson College
Massachusetts Cultural Council
National Endowment for the Arts

Co-Publisher: $10,000 for two lifetime subscriptions and acknowledgment in the journal for five years.

Council: $3,500 for two lifetime subscriptions and acknowledgment in the journal for three years.

Patron: $1,000 for a lifetime subscription and acknowledgment in the journal for two years.

Friend: $500 for acknowledgment in the journal for one year.

ALICE HOFFMAN
Introduction: Storyteller

Not long ago, I met a woman in her eighties in the parking lot of a library in Florida. I had been at the library to give a reading, and one member of the audience waited for me after everyone else had left, despite the brutal, engulfing heat. The stranger was attractive, elegant, and well-dressed, but clearly emotional. She took me aside, asking to speak with me alone for a moment. As we stood in the shade of a banyan tree, she leaned in close, as if she had a great secret, one she could share with me alone.

She whispered that she had a story.

This was not an entirely unusual occurrence. As I traveled around the country, speaking about my novels and my life as a writer, I was frequently approached by people who had stories of their own, ones they wished to disclose to me in the hopes that I might write them down. Often those stories were the histories of their lives, narratives they themselves had been unable to express in a way that adequately conveyed their experiences and emotions. Because they had not told their stories, they had been forced to carry them; it was as if the untold tales had been stored in backpacks they could not set down, or tied to the soles of their feet with black thread. They were haunted.

I gave advice to such people: writers' workshops, classes at local colleges, summer programs for beginning memoirists, books that might help them write their own narratives. For some these suggestions were worthwhile, but others needed more help; their stories were somehow trapped inside them, and however powerful these stories might be, they could not write them down. Over time, I came to see these people as if each were a book, a volume that had yet to be written, but which all the same remained real and vibrant and affecting. The stories burned inside them, the fervor flaming ever stronger as years went by. Stories define who we are and who we wish to be. They warn, they remind, they cut so deeply they can leave a scar. If left untold, they can linger and grow heavier, for every tale is made for two: The teller and the listener. The writer and the reader.

In the scorching parking lot in Florida, beneath the shade of the banyan tree's extraordinary boughs, the stranger who had waited so patiently began to confide details of her childhood during the Holocaust. She had lived a secret existence, and now, as she began to reveal some of the details of her life to me, she seemed to grow younger, a beautiful, damaged girl who was forced to keep her identity secret. She spoke of fields of lavender, of stone cellars and ice-cold nights, and of the parents she had lost and yearned for even now, as we stood together in the heat, an old woman and a writer who would be old soon enough. The past shimmered around us, palpable, laden with sorrow.

My stranger said there was no time to waste. She felt that her age and the circumstances of her health, along with the decline of others who had survived the Holocaust as children, meant whatever stories had been left untold would soon disappear. She'd waited to speak to me because she wanted me to write hers. If her history was not expressed and examined, it might disappear. If her story was left untold, my stranger feared, the world she had known would disappear when she did, her struggle and her journey worthless if they went unremembered.

Although I had compassion for her plight, I insisted I hadn't the right to tell another person's story, especially the story of a survivor of the Holocaust. My stranger, however, disagreed. She took my hand, held it, and said, "I give you permission."

I give you permission, to imagine, to create a world, to make history come alive, to take my secret and add your own. I give you permission to take on my life and write fiction, to add details that have vanished from mind, to take the map of my soul and use it as a beginning and an endpoint. For me, it was particularly meaningful that this beautiful, aging stranger had sought a novelist rather than a writer of nonfiction and that she believed the truth of her personal experience would best be served by fiction. Certainly, as a reader, I had always discovered the deepest truths in fiction; it was through reading novels that I learned about the world, a world not only of fact but of imagination and emotion. That is what my stranger wanted, what we receive from poetry and from fiction, not a list of real items, but the chart of an emotional landscape. For her, that was the truth.

I owe my stranger a story, one I hope someday to tell so that I might do justice to her experience, but for now I simply owe her a debt of gratitude. She gave me a gift on the day that we met, the right to take any story and make it my own. Most young writers are told to write what they know. I disagree. If you can imagine it, you can tell it. It is within the realm of the imagination that we find our truest stories, stories of the heart and of the soul. We take the world that we know and we reshape it. In doing so we see behind veils, beneath doors, through the dark glass of the past. What we are left with is a circle of shining light, a creation that is both the miracle and the charm, something one must share to give it any worth at all, a story.

PAULA BOHINCE
Everywhere I Went That Spring, I Was Alone

In the single room of a bathtub, humming "Love
Me Tender" to hear a sullen human
voice. Then after,

fainting in slow motion to the tile. Succumbing
to steam and waking, on my
own, drowsy as a rose.

Mailing a letter and waiting, empty, beside a hornet's
thumb-small home, fit inside the lip
of the mailbox. The hornet

each day startled less by the sudden thunder
of the falling drawbridge, the cymbal
of sunshine let in.

In the kitchen, beside the toaster, crying unabashedly
into dishtowels as I timed my meal
and kept company the cool

block of butter in its iridescent silver, the blunt
knife, the beveled glass that carried
my milk. Alone

when it began to hail one afternoon. A miracle
suspending the cottage in darkness. Alone
taking a photograph

of the glory and alone when the pearly
melt returned the grass to ordinary June. Everywhere
those months my nose buzzed

from crying. Quivered so unlike the hornet, pitiless
in her work. Bleeding intermittently
into my dress hem, how beautiful I became

then, ringed by brown flowers. More
hornet than my hornet friend, alone in her own
collapsing universe.

RUTH BLANK
Tomato Season

After Samuel died and I had to move up north to live with Faith and her husband Dan, I got rid of almost everything I owned. Not that I wanted to, but there was no space in their drafty house near the river for their things and my things too. I really only had a few good pieces, a mahogany breakfront that we had in the front hall and the cherry dining room set that could seat a crowd. I hated giving them up, but that's what had happened to my life.

I brought with me my secretary, though, a piece that had been my Aunt Ida's and that held Samuel's theology books in its upper shelves and had the little drop-down desk where I could write my letters. I had to bring my own bedding and linens because Faith liked to use percale sheets and things that needed no ironing, as though she couldn't afford help. It's not the way she grew up, but you can't tell your child what to do when you're living in her home.

Faith came south for Samuel's funeral—Dan stayed up north with their boy, Wendell. The elders were in a big hurry to turn over my home to the new minister. No matter that I lived there thirty-seven years, that I'd had their wives in for tea or sherry countless times and kept it up as a reflection on them and their parish. I was out without so much as a question as to how I might get by. I never asked Faith if I could move in with her. And she never asked me, either. She just said, with that hard set of her jaw, "You're going to have to part with this big furniture."

When they picked me up from the airport on my first day up north, Dan did not come. Wendell hid behind his mother's legs as we waited for my bags. I pulled the Raggedy Andy that had been Faith's out of my carry-on and tried to hand it to him, but he just clutched his mother's calves and said "Why is she so fat?" I didn't try giving him that precious doll again, and when I saw Faith stroking his long brown hair instead of punishing him, I wished I could go right back to Greenville, house or no house.

They put me in what they called "the sewing room," with no closet and a day bed with noisy springs. I had to keep most of my belongings put away, and most of my clothes in a grip under the day bed, but I didn't complain. With the pitched ceiling, my secretary had to practically sit in the middle of the room, right there for me to trip over. I'm sure Faith wanted me to let her get rid of it, but I'd be black and blue before turning it over to a junk dealer.

I didn't have much to do with Dan. Faith and Wendell were all that we had in common, so we said very little to each other. If we were ever alone in a room, it fell to me to get a conversation going. I'd mention the privets at the end of their property, that maybe they ought to be cut back to let a little more afternoon sun in the yard, or I'd bring up Wendell's quiet nature and I'd get one- or two-word answers from Dan. He almost never looked at me. It seemed as though he wanted to pretend I wasn't there and if he actually looked at me, he'd have to face the fact of me. Most times, I stayed very quiet and listened to where he was going in the house so that I could be in a different room.

The one thing I asked of him was to let me have a little piece of the yard, a patch near the crumbling cottage in the back that got midday sun so that I could put in a tomato garden and maybe grow some nice ones in the few weeks that is the growing season up here.

Even though spring came late where they lived, I spent time outdoors when it was possible so that I could stay out of their way. I noticed some feral cats that wandered by through the privets, stealthy and curious too. We always had a house cat or two in Greenville. I asked Faith to get me a couple of cans of tuna at the store, and if she thought they were for my lunch, so be it. I was able to urge the two scruffy, skinny cats to come around to the back of the house for a snack, and after a few feedings, they let me pet them. Faith didn't say anything, though I'm sure she knew what I was doing.

It turned out Dan had delicate sinuses. Even a few cat hairs on my clothes when I came inside set him off. I tried brushing myself off best as I could, but he kept hacking that little dry cough—not saying anything, but making his point.

So they offered me what they were pleased to call "the cottage" at the edge of the lawn, close to the river. I had to traipse through the mud just to come to the house for dinner. As musty and moldy as that little place was, I at least got to make friends with the two cats. I named them Smudge and Dora—Smudge, the whitish one with a splash of gray on his face, and Dora, the same coffee-and-cream color as our dear maid, Dora, who was with us for almost thirty years until Samuel died. Those cats let me pet them, and if I stayed still, one might jump into my lap.

The cottage bed was no better than the noisy day bed; there was always a little tackiness to my good sheets, but I slept better there, not having to listen to Faith and Dan whisper at night, trying to keep me from hearing them. It was hard to tell whether there was any fondness in their whispering, and it became tiresome to try to pick up a word or a tone of voice.

I spent a lot of time alone in that cottage except for the occasional visit from the boy, who became used to me, or so it seemed. He liked to open the cans of food for the cats. He was too afraid to pet them, since he saw they were poison to his father.

Of all the strange things in that cottage—a bathtub sunken into the floor so you had to risk your neck getting into it, and walls that sweated nicotine from former smoking inhabitants—the strangest thing was the electric can opener built into the wall. Someone made everything else in that cottage as inconvenient and nasty as possible, but they saw to it that it was easy to open a can. Well, it did amuse Wendell, and he gave me a little company now and then, even though the child was as hard to get to know as anyone I'd ever met.

On a Saturday in March when the ground had pretty much thawed for the season, Dan dug out a few square yards of ground in front of the privets, built a couple of raised beds, tossed in a bag of topsoil, and hooked up a PVC pipe sprinkler system that attached to a faucet outside the cottage. He never said he built that garden for me, but I knew I'd be the only one tending it.

"Try to keep those cats from crapping in there," was all that he said by way of telling me it was ready.

It was a good workable garden from day one, and I thanked him plenty and promised beautiful Early Girls by Fourth of July and a summer full of Beefsteaks and Brandywines. No one seemed too excited, but I had never spent a summer without tomatoes and I wasn't about to just because Samuel died and I had to live in this cottage with the damp furniture and the long winter.

Faith didn't seem to remember the beautiful garden I kept in Greenville. She would have been content to buy from the store or the farm stand, but maybe I could get the boy to enjoy a tomato still warm off the vine. And maybe I could get him to pet Smudge or Dora instead of just opening cans for them. Maybe I could get him to say more than a sentence at a time to me.

Wendell came across the squishy yard on the day I was planting. He wore galoshes with his dungarees tucked in and a Philadelphia Flyers leather jacket that looked like a big waste of money to me because he was bound to outgrow it before he even really knew what game that team played. He carried a dirty spade with him. I couldn't tell whether his mother sent him down the lawn to me or whether he came on his own, and I didn't ask.

I made the furrows and Wendell put the seeds in the soil where I showed him, and then I let him jam the stakes in where he had planted. That seemed to be his favorite part, the only thing I'd ever seen him do with much gusto. He was quiet, as usual, concentrating so hard on his work that he started humming.

"Well. Won't you be happy when these beauties get big and ripe and you can slice 'em up for supper?"

"I'm not allowed to slice," he said. Of course he wasn't.

"I can show you how to slice."

He looked me in the eye for what might have been the first time ever. "You can?"

I made him take his galoshes off, even though tracking in mud couldn't have made the place look any worse. I sat him down at the little table in what served as a kitchen and got the utility knife out of the drawer.

"How can I cut a tomato? They haven't growed yet."

"Let's see," I looked around. I didn't keep much in that cottage. "How about a lemon?"

"I don't eat lemons."

"You're not eating. You're learning how to slice."

I put the knife in his right hand. He didn't grip it naturally. His hand was limp, as though he thought his mother was watching and he didn't want her to think he actually wanted to hold the knife. I wrapped my hand around his and positioned his index finger and thumb so he could maneuver. I had to practically squeeze his small, soft fingers to get him to hold on. Then I put the chopping board in front of him and set the lemon on the board so that it would be easy.

I stood above him and held the lemon with my left hand and guided his with my right. He refused to grip it himself, so I wrapped my hand a little tighter around his.

"Ow," he said.

"C'mon," I said. "It's easy."

"No it's not. I can't slice."

"Don't be silly."

I don't know whose hand was actually holding the knife, but I brought our hands together in line with the lemon to make the first slice. Wendell tried to grab his hand away, and when he jerked, he twisted the knife so that it landed deep in my left hand. In an instant, blood appeared on the lemon.

We both dropped the knife, and before I could say a word, Wendell had run out the door and headed up the lawn to his house. I turned on the cold water and ran it over my hand, watching the watery blood run onto the cracked porcelain. I could see from the gash that it might need a stitch or two. The pain was clean and sharp and close to the bone. I might need to go on up to the house and get Faith or Dan to drive me to a doctor.

But first, I ran the bloody knife under water, dried it, and put it back in the drawer. I rinsed the lemon and placed it in the fruit bowl. Light was pouring into the cottage on all of the secondhand furniture and on my beautiful secretary that I hadn't used since the day I moved. My hand was throbbing and bleeding through the paper towel that I had wrapped around it. I knew I should tend to it, and I would, and I'd see to Wendell and quiet the silly fears his parents put in him, but the cottage was warm and I was tired, so before I did anything else, I lay down on the damp couch in my new home and just rested.

The drowsiness that took me over was pleasant, and when Faith came busting in the door—she almost never came down to the cottage—I thought someone must be hurt.

"Wendell is hysterical. He says he stabbed you."

I sat up. I was coming out of my sleepy state and beginning to remember a mishap with the knife, and even though I heard what she said, Faith looked so angry, I thought for a moment that I had stabbed Wendell.

"Oh, for Christ sake," she said. "Look at your hand." The second she said it, I felt the throbbing. The bloody paper towel was bunched between my thumb and forefinger. "Let me look at it." She grabbed my hand and pulled the paper towel off. It stung where the blood had glued the paper to the gash. "Honestly," she said. "He's crying his head off up there and Dan is not pleased."

"Well, I wouldn't want Dan to be bothered," I said quietly.

"You need to have this looked at. Thanks a lot, Mom. I don't have enough to do today without having to run you to the emergency room."

"You stay with your family," I said. "I can call a cab."

"Sure you will," she said. "Put a fresh paper towel around it and come up to the car. And don't forget your insurance card." She looked around the room like an inspector. "Jesus. That secretary needs to go."

Faith let the screen door slam behind her. Like everything else in that cottage, the screen was askew, and with the door open, I could see that the flies and mosquitoes were going to plague me all summer. I watched Faith disappear into her house, and then I sat back down on the couch with my hand up to keep it above my heart. I wished I had Dora to take care of me. If she were here, I could count on her to wrap the cut just right and fix me a nice bowl of gumbo.

After Faith left for college, when she came home for breaks, she would roll her eyes when I asked Dora to do something for her, like fix her breakfast. Now, of course, Faith did all of her own cooking and cleaning, and she seemed to have forgotten how she used to tie Dora's apron strings around her own waist so that the two of them were attached. Dora let little Faith walk behind her, attached to her body with crisply starched cotton ties as she went about her work. Faith would say, "I'm the maid, Momma. Watch me clean up."

I could hear the car starting up in the driveway, but I didn't get my purse and I didn't move. It occurred to me that I hadn't watered the seeds that Wendell and I just planted, and if they didn't get watered today, all that work would be wasted. I went outside to turn on the faucet that would supply the drip system, and I saw those cats—fattened up since I started feeding them—digging in the fresh, rich soil. It appeared that now they were mine.

MARTHA COLLINS
In White

a white-trunked white-
limbed white-leafed tree

white petals sepals white
stamens pistils bees inside

a white woman pure
white body skin hair

white eyes white
lips nipples blood

white grass for the white
stones of this white dream

MARTHA COLLINS
That Night, I

carried a baby
heart in my pocket

neat pink packet
that kept beating a

quiet music or
calling machine

with no reception
except in my hand

that reached from time
to time in my pocket

and cradled that only
connection to what

might have been or
was it to what might be

KERRY JAMES EVANS
Blackbird

There are thirteen ways to look at a blackbird, but my backyard is not
    a blackbird,
        and I am not Wallace Stevens,
but I make do with an air conditioning unit and the remnants of an
    entertainment center,
        the cherry wood stain fading into sod.

I look down at this plot of land like I look at cornfields from a plane,
    the reordering
        of things: cities in patches
of clover, my folding chair the arch swaying in St. Louis, the smoker
    a memory
        of my ancestors

pulling pork shoulder in Carolina, my ancestors hooking ham in the
    meat house.
        Look how the memory
changes course. The bluebird fusses with the field mouse. They are a
    government
        maintained by a falcon

searing the air with mating calls, another passing plane I notice from
    the passenger window.
        Fire ants drive to work
below me, groceries on their backs, bypassing juniper berries and twigs,
    a dump site
        for a squirrel's muscadine.

I am in thirteen places at once, looking off a concrete slab, my cooler
    half-filled
        with beer and watered-down ice,

the bottle of Pinot Grigio that turned my wife into a groggy mess. She
    threw the cork
        into the yard.

My little silo in a cornfield carved into squares. The air conditioning
    unit clicks on
        and hums
like the state capitol down the road. In that room an energy lobbyist
    hikes my rates.
        The bill will be mailed this month.

Here, I am the blackbird on the wire and the plane that dropped me
    in Birmingham,
        Alabama when I
was a child—when the landscape looked the same from any height:
    pine or sycamore,
        the roof of the house

I helped my father build after the fall, politics and farmland as small
    now as they were
        when I wore
sweatpants to school, and the yard will grow smaller as I age. The
    plane crash lands
        in the Black Warrior,

my baptism, where the catfish grab my back fat, where they grab the
    bones
        in my ankles,
and this concrete slab: my tombstone sinking into a riverbed of gravel,
    the iron gate
        leaning over this roaring grave.

Kerry James Evans

JAMES FRANCO
The Deer

I always sat in the back of Mr. Kim's algebra class. He was very enthusiastic about algebra. I drew a picture of me sticking my dick into Rex's blond dreamgirl. Rex was on the other side of the room. I folded the paper and wrote Rex on the top, and told this ugly girl, Andrea Blatt, to pass it along. She passed it to another girl who passed it, and everyone passed it until it got to Rex. He couldn't tell it was supposed to be his dreamgirl. He laughed out loud. Mr. Kim looked at him, and then looked at me. People tell me I look like Warren Beatty, maybe that's why he was staring.

We went out and got croissants and cold chocolate milk in little cartons. We discussed our Santa Cruz trip. Seth Cranston was with us. In eighth grade we called him "Naps." Then one day, this white kid we didn't know called him Naps, and Seth beat the kid into a coma. Seth went to juvenile hall. While he was in there, he stabbed another kid with a pencil seventeen times and it was in the *Palo Alto Weekly*. Finally he got out. No one called him Naps anymore.

We were all across the street at Town and Country, in the parking lot where everyone smokes if they're not smoking in the bat cave. I have a brown 1987 Buick LeSabre station wagon. My dad gave it to me. It's a boat with a thin plastic steering wheel and a faux-wood dash. It is as slow as a cloud. My dad is rich, but he's cheap. All the little skaters were around, smoking and doing ollies. Seth heard our Santa Cruz plan and he asked if he could go. We said no, it was a private thing. Seth was pissed. He stood up and pushed one of the skaters off his board. Seth got on the board and did a bad ollie on it. Then he rode it into the street and jumped off. It broke under a car's wheels on Embarcadero. The kid, whose board it was, called Seth Naps. I choked on my chocolate milk. Seth walked over to the kid. All the kid's friends backed away. They all had wide eyes. Rex and I sat on the curb, watching and laughing. I had this thick, coated feeling in my throat from the chocolate milk, the Camel cigarettes, and the rest of the croissant I was chewing on, and I was still a little high.

The little skater had long black bangs that hung straight down in front. He wore a skater outfit: baggy pants and a baggy black T-shirt. For a second, the kid was trying to act tough, but Seth grabbed him by his bangs in the front, and pulled his face downward so he was bending over. The kid grabbed Seth's hand and was kicking at Seth, but he couldn't reach. Then Seth whipped the kid's head up and back in a violent jerk. The kid was almost crying. There was nothing he could do because Seth was so much bigger. Then the kid fell on his ass, but Seth was still holding his bangs. The kid was sitting there, holding Seth's hand and screaming, and Seth was stepping on the kid's stomach, and then on his neck and face, while still pulling his bangs. Rex and I were dying because the kid was pulling at Seth's leg to make him stop and he started pulling off Seth's sweatpants, and it was making Seth madder. Seth was telling the kid to stop pulling off his pants. Then Seth's tightie-whities were showing and they looked yellow.

The driver that ran over the skateboard pulled into the parking lot. He was in this stupid brown station wagon, just like mine. He started yelling at Seth to stop, and we all yelled back at him. We told him to get in the car and to get the fuck out of there. Even the other little skaters were yelling at him. The only one not yelling at him was the kid on the ground because he was still struggling with Seth. Then Rex and I threw our chocolate milk at the car. He got back in his car and said he was going to call the police.

We all went back to class.

I had biology third period. We were dissecting piglets. It was sick. My partner was Meena Cohen. She screeched when I cut open the piglet. I cut off the pig's head, even though I wasn't supposed to, and she screeched a whole bunch more. There were a lot of screeches all over the room, so Meena wasn't alone.

Right after I cut off the pig's head, Simpson came by, on his stupid bicycle. He was security on campus. Assistant football coach. He told Ms. Johnson that he was taking me to the office. I was holding the pig head by the ear when Ms. Johnson told me to go with Simpson. I walked out with the head behind my back. We walked across the lawn. Simpson was walking his mountain bike and his big ass in his little shorts. I dropped the pig head in the bushes before we went up the office steps. I didn't get in trouble. Seth got suspended. Dean Schneiderman told me I was mean-spirited for laughing at the skater's pain. By the time I got out, fourth period was half over. Simpson was gone. I grabbed the pig head out of the bushes. It had some dirt on the cut neck. I went over to the spot between the theater and the office, where nobody goes. I smoked three cigarettes. I put the cigarettes out on the pig's eyelids. He looked angry. Then it was lunch.

At lunch we all went over to Terry Price's. I saw him walking to the parking lot and he told me to come over. I drove over in my brown LeSabre. Terry lived pretty close to school, and his parents were never there. There were a whole bunch of us at the house. We smoked pot on his balcony. I found a chain in Terry's room that went with some fake dog tags. Everyone went downstairs and made bologna sandwiches with white bread and yellow mustard. I didn't eat mine.

While everyone was eating, I took the dog tags off the chain and cut little holes in the pig's ears with a kitchen knife, and then I put the chain through the holes. I had a pig head necklace.

We stayed at Terry's for fifth period. Then Danny Camillo came over and sold me some acid. I got five tabs for twenty bucks. It was Felix the Cat brand. There were these little Felix the Cat heads on all the tabs. I didn't want to go back to school, so I went home. I hung the pig head from my rear view mirror.

I had my own apartment because my dad owned the building. My dad and mom were on the same floor as me, and my little sister lived with them. My older brother also had his own apartment. I called my place the Punisher pad. I had a Punisher poster on the wall. It was a white skull, without a jaw, against a black background. I took one tab of acid and I watched porn on my couch for an hour. Rex walked in and I gave him a tab of acid. We had time, so we watched a movie, *Less than Zero*. It was bad. Rex said that he read the book and it was better. I had to get up and get some water on my face. I went to the bathroom and I couldn't find myself in the mirror. Then I found myself. I didn't look like Warren Beatty at all.

I peeked out the door to where Rex was sitting on the couch. He had his back to me, and he was doing big whooping laughs at the television.

I didn't come out of the bathroom for a long time. I sat on the toilet. I saw space and time.

I came out. Rex was lying down on the floor. He was watching *Full House*. I was still looking in the mirror even though it was in the other room.

"I'm not driving you out to Santa Cruz like this," I said. "We'll get Naps to drive."

We called Seth. He was at home. He said he wasn't supposed to go out because he got suspended. Rex told him to fuck off, and to drive us to Santa Cruz.

"I thought it was a private party."

"Well it was," I said. "But now it's not."

There was a silence on the other end. Then Seth said, "OK, I'll be right over. I have to ride my bike." Seth came over, and I was trying to keep him quiet because of my dad being in the next apartment even though he never really heard anything.

I didn't want Seth to know that we were on acid. You couldn't trust him when he was high. After a bit he said, "Are you guys high?" Rex and I were sitting right next to each other on the couch. Rex looked at me, but said nothing. It looked like there was a baby goldfish in his eye. I turned back to Seth and told him we were just high on weed. He asked for some and I said it was all gone.

I didn't even want to go to Santa Cruz.

Seth drove us. I was in the front seat and Rex was in the back. The little piglet head hung from the rearview. We drove on the 17 and it's really windy and it goes up this mountain, through all these woods before it dumps you out at the beach. It was dark, and I just watched all the dark trees go by. We listened to Doctor Dre and Tupac and DJ Quick. When the bass hit hard I could see it. The trees shook to the bass. I closed my eyes and there were white bass circles.

My dad and mom used to take me and my older brother and my younger sister out to Santa Cruz. We'd always go to a beach called Capitola. In my memories, it's beautiful. There were these different colored adobe houses, right on the beach. We'd rent one out and stay for a week during the summer. There was this lake next to the beach, with a great big railroad bridge over it, and it was so high and big and black. Like a bridge you'd see in a train set. I once saw this Western, and this guy had to jump off a bridge like that because he was on the run. He had an arrow in his chest and he couldn't pull it out, so he broke it off and went around with the point stuck inside him for the whole film.

My family and I would take the 17 through the woods. About halfway up the mountain, there were these two large cat sculptures. They were guarding a gate in the trees. When I was young, I would look for them every time we went. Even when I was older and was getting in a lot of trouble, I would still look for them.

We passed the cats in the dark. I saw them, looming, white and large and hazy. I dreamed about the road, I must have been asleep for a bit, and then Seth and Rex were yelling at each other. Seth was freaking out. He saw I was awake and he started clawing me. "What the fuck is going on?" I said. We kept yelling the question at each other as we wrestled. I checked my pockets.

"Where the fuck is my acid," I said. "I ate it all!" he yelled.

"He's fucking gone," said Rex from the back seat. While I was asleep, Rex had fallen asleep too. Seth had found my acid and had been driving around for two hours through the woods. "He's out of his mind."

Seth was blank, and dumb. "What happened?" I said.

"I think we hit a deer," said Rex.

"Fuck you," I said. This road was beautiful. I knew that, even if I couldn't see it through the dark. Seth didn't say anything. He just looked straight ahead and drove. There was a whirring sound, like something was dragging at the front of the car. I opened the door and the thick whirring got louder. Then the whirring stopped, and it was just the rushing sound of air. I shut the door.

"I think we're OK," I said. Nobody answered me.

I had Seth pull the car over. There was something stuck to the front of the grill, but I didn't look too closely. We got in, Rex climbed into the front, and I drove the rest of the way. The pig head dangled from the rear view. He had his little burned-out eyes and his little tongue sticking out. Rex grabbed him and threw him out the window.

We passed the two big cat statues. On our left this time.

I got us down to the 101 and then north to Palo Alto. I knew exactly where I was going. There's a public parking structure across from my father's building. I parked on the top level. Rex and I got out, and Seth got out of the back, and we went to the front of the car. The car was under a tall light. In the grill, there was a hoof. It had bent the metal. There was a big part of the leg left, all the way past the knee.

I took the skinny part in my hands, the bloody part under my armpit, and I yanked the hoof out of the metal. I threw the leg over the side of the parking structure.

BONNIE FRIEDMAN
Coming of Age in Book Country

I knew I was back in New York when I saw children walking to school with books open in their hands. I'd lived away for fifteen years. Now down the streets of Brooklyn they drifted, novels spread wide between their palms, the actual world comprising a mere running margin of asphalt and high-heeled shoes and honking cars. The massive knapsacks sagging off their backs seemed a wise precaution against the danger of the children floating right off into the realms of imagination that lured them down the street transfixed, one foot set absently in front of the next.

I'd been the same way not long ago. Growing up in the Bronx, I read myself to P.S. 24 in the morning and read myself home each afternoon. My best friends were fanatical readers—Emily, a science wizard who used wads of pink Kleenex for bookmarks, and Stacy, who, despite our apartment life, penned guides on the best way to lay out an herb garden and how to ride horses in proper English style, ramrod straight, a moss-velvet riding helmet on one's head. She read me her work leaning against the cyclone fence in the J.H.S. 141 schoolyard near the kids slamming handballs.

It seemed perfectly natural to us that our parents owned novels set in our own city—*The Chosen; A Tree Grows in Brooklyn; Where Are You Going? Out. What Are You Doing? Nothing;* and a bevy of Mafia tales. Even then we sensed that the city was always being reinvented and pulped. The streets were jackhammered constantly; we looked for squares of fresh cement in which to finger our names. New York was book country because it was half real and half imagined, as were we ourselves. Hadn't a storybook boy spent the night at the Metropolitan Museum? Didn't my brother tell me about a young man in a novel who worried about the ducks in Central Park—where did they go in the winter? After that, I worried about them too.

Every book was a book of spells, and we longed to transform ourselves. My friends and I were like James Gatz, yearning to climb up the moonlight ladder to where blond gods quaff nectar in spangled rooms. How tired we were of long division and ink splotches, of tedious pretests and retests, and of being chosen almost last in gym games. The girls chosen first read *Seventeen*, not *The Island of the Blue Dolphins*. And they smelled of Herbal Essences, not the stone halls of the Cloisters, where we drifted about in states of mystical transport on Sunday afternoons.

We longed for adventure, and the revelation of one's true inner identity, which had nothing to do with the face in the mirror or popularity or grades, but with the crown-tips of letters themselves and the perpetual twilight in the original growth forest maintained deep in the Botanical Gardens—leaf-mold scent drifting up, shadow doorways appearing and vanishing.

My friends and I passed around *Act One* by Moss Hart, a Bronx boy who ended up living at the Waldorf. His wife, Kitty Carlisle on *To Tell the Truth*, always clasped an invisible martini in her hand. You'd never know she'd grown up Horowitz. My friend Stacy's father brought us all to the Tiki Room at the Plaza for her eleventh birthday, and we ate with chopsticks and sipped virgin pineapple blender drinks, and the reek of the Bunsen burners was the most sophisticated scent I'd ever inhaled.

The other patrons glowered. We were a table of shrieky girls. I longed to be a grown-up with a long white cashmere dress like the woman across the room, for a man to notice me through the candlelight. And yet the theatricality of the marble-corridored hotel made me consider the presence of its invisible author—the person who put the waiters in tuxes and who arranged the palms in the Palm Court, where a storybook girl ate lunch. Even then it seemed clear that Manhattan was composed and calculated, like a wildly concocted plot, but that I would get to play a part in it merely by maturing, as if the city were something I would grow into like a shoe.

Every other issue of *New York* magazine in those days—the early seventies—seemed to carry a cover story about a housewife with a secret life. This one hung out with drug addicts. This one posed for girlie pix. It seemed clear that to live in New York was to have a secret life, and it was only a matter of getting older and finding out what yours would be. Who needed the unconscious? New York was the unconscious. Waiting for my friend Emily outside Hunter Junior High, I asked a man "Do you have the time?" "If you've got the place," he answered. I swiveled my head away and let my eyes follow a city bus, as though I didn't understand.

But I knew what his words meant, and I was flattered and frightened. What if I'd said: "I don't have the place, but do you?" What would have happened then? If you could dream it, it could happen in New York—that seemed keenly true to me at thirteen. My friends and I carried our secret lives before us like emblems; we read them as we walked to school and read them on the bus. The city itself was a library of apartment buildings, each with stories spooling down echoey corridors and with dialogue leaking through the plasterboard. Often we put a cup to the wall so we could hear it better. "Shhh!" we'd say to our families, glaring, fingers to our lips, ears shoved hard against the glass.

My friends and I read only novels. Nonfiction did not exist, despite Stacy's pamphlets on how to live the cultivated British life. It wasn't until late in junior high, when a friend showed me a book outlining the five ballet positions, that I considered the possibility that volumes stuffed with facts might actually be real books. But what sad books they seemed! How thin—no matter their sprawl and heft. Books of fact all seemed like math, as if a thousand wood pointers were banging against a thousand chalkboards on which were inscribed life's rock-hard realities. How frightening! I was terrible at school. I was, in fact, terrible at everything except reading, which at the time seemed about as useful as whittling.

Years later—my first job out of college—I found myself working on a definitive book of facts, *The Guinness Book of World Records*. The country of books had sucked me up for good. I sat beside the proofreader on the 26th floor of a deco skyscraper and read copy aloud to him. The man with the longest fingernails, which twirled from his fingertips like paper party noisemakers. The man who'd drifted the longest time at sea. The Siamese twins scissoring away from each other, dapper, married to sisters. Out the office window the sunset laid siege to New Jersey. It hovered from 3:00 p.m. on in shades of hibiscus and tangerine. I didn't want to hear it was pollution, something the production manager felt obliged to explain. I was so happy to have a job in Manhattan involving books.

The proofreader and I ate dried pineapple chunks and cashews from brown paper sleeves we'd bought at lunch. He told me that I resembled a young Leslie Caron. I was obscurely attracted to him, and went over to his apartment on West 94th, and watched a sea of glittering cockroaches recede miraculously into the walls, and then sat on his mattress on the floor and gazed at Fred Astaire dancing with Ginger Rogers through a TV screen thick with haze. Women's faces peered down from the apartment walls, dozens of them ripped from magazines and taped three feet from the floor: Bette Davis, Jean Harlow, all seeming to smolder with disapproval, as if his superego were female, as if he would feel its eyes on him even in the dark.

"I'll never make a play for you," said the proofreader to me at a Beefsteak Charlie's on 34th Street. "Don't expect that I will."

But I was still so averse to facts I had no idea what he meant. The next time I came over he showed me his feather collection—bluebird feathers, wild turkey feathers, and many feathers of unknown origin, tawny, with a triangular eye at the top, as if an inky pen had been allowed to bleed. He kept them crammed in a brown paper lunch bag in his closet, so many that the sides of the bag were round. For how long had he been collecting them? "Draw the feather across your upper lip," he instructed. "Doesn't it feel nice?" "Oh, it does," I answered. Then he walked me to the subway. An enormous sadness seemed to fill the night. I thought wildly: "I should stay with him until he's happy!" I thought this mad thought even as he waved to me from the top of the stairs. How I would have liked to dash up to him! How I would have liked to touch the bearded texture of his cheek!

His grandfather had been an illustrious publisher: the first to publish James Joyce in the United States. This heritage weighed heavily on the proofreader, who disbelieved himself worthy of it. The proofreader himself was easier to talk to than almost any man I'd ever met. He carried a Channel 13 tote with orange print on canvas, and took me to see *Casablanca* at the Thalia, and he told me about New Orleans, where he'd grown up fatherless, but always this wild melancholy seemed to throb around us, and it glued me to him. I kept thinking that if I could just get closer or stay longer, the melancholy would disperse.

One day, the proofreader was fired. He'd been proofing fewer and fewer galley pages. When he averaged less than two a day, he was dismissed. Meanwhile, I'd been promoted to editing children's joke books and puzzle books. Soon I departed for Boston, which was cheaper and where I thought I might at last learn to write. A decade later, visiting my parents, I saw the proofreader on the platform at 42nd Street, about to board the No. 1 uptown. "Oh!" I gasped, but didn't exert myself to call his name.

He looked so familiar I had the ridiculous feeling that I'd be seeing him again soon anyway, which of course I never did. But our strange romance—watching dance movies, reading aloud the jerky and now antiquated language of proofing (*caps, ques, bang*), and the strong scent of Mitchum aftershave contained in his bathroom—all returned to me.

How long I had remained in ignorance!—even after he told me about a very close male friend of his who liked to dress up in stockings and brassiere. Even after he told me that he'd never had a girlfriend in his adulthood. He had announced himself to me as explicitly as he could bear, but I maintained my perverse innocence, and felt forever that we were on the edge of a breakthrough of intimacy that would somehow resolve our mutual melancholy. I refused to read his secret life, which he had come to New York to live.

My own was resolved through the mirrored halls of sentences. I found myself in prose. And he, I suspect, discovered himself in the meeting places of the city. He phoned me once, a few months after he was fired. "I've called to tell you something," he said. "I've joined a weekly group for people like me. I can't elaborate. But I'm much happier now." Even then—it was 1981—I had no idea what he meant. I simply refused to believe, of course, what I already knew, which was that the erotic haze around us would always remain as unconsummatable as the romance of a reader for a character in a book.

After I hung up, I stood there with my hand on my parents' mustard-colored phone, pondering what he meant by "weekly group for people like me." My mother glanced up from her *Short Story International*. The No. 100 bus hauled by up 239th Street. Both my ignorance and my insight came from bookishness, I knew. How much bigger my life might be if I could thrust aside my books! And yet I couldn't really picture a life bigger than a life in books. I'd grown up in book country and it was where I meant to live. I picked up "Hills Like White Elephants," which I happened to be reading even though I had no idea what it was about. What did it mean, for the woman to have an operation to "let the air in"? And why were the man and the woman in the story in such bad moods? I needed to read everything much more closely, I suddenly felt with an urgency that made my head pound. I could scarcely bear the weight of my own ignorance. Try to understand, try to understand, I told myself, bending over the book again. Why was I so obtuse?

I stared at the type so closely that it seemed a pillared temple-front colonnade I could enter. The mattress creaked in my father's bedroom as he turned, drowsing, taking a break from his worries. My mother flipped a page of her magazine. The world around me was bewildering, unkempt, shifting, repetitive, and with no index or glossary, no chapter titles. But although there was much I didn't understand in my reading, there was much that I did. I recognized the girl saying fanciful, clever things—performing. And the longing of the young man to stay at the bar where the people are "reasonable." "What is your group?" I wanted to ask the proofreader. "How are you happier? Why are you calling me?" Afraid to demand the answers of life, I bent closer to the page. The city itself waited patiently, constructing and destroying and raising itself again at the end of the subway line. Sitting at my way station, I realized that an era of my life had ended. It was possible to change one's fate; one could be happier. How? The book told me the answer, but I was not yet willing to pay the price it stipulated, and so I kept on reading, although I was sick at heart.

Bonnie Friedman 33

URSULA K. LE GUIN
Hour of the Changes

A wild early April strangeness,
crazier than any autumn evening,
mild air full of flooding wind,
motions of storming branches,
a queer, creaky, crying sound
way off, as the rain advances—
What's that?—thud of thunder?
a big tree going down?
the sound of the untime after?
No, only the hour of the changes,
swift, oceanic,
smelling of hyacinth, ozone, daphne.

URSULA K. LE GUIN
Lorca's Duende

The duende got into my head
by the back staircase,
a gypsy girl-child dressed in red
with an old man's face.

My bedroom turned bitter cold.
There were banging noises,
loud knockings in between the walls.
Things left their places.

My comb crawled across the bureau,
clicking like castanets.
My grandmother's ivory-backed mirror
cracked itself into bits.

Get out of my head, old child.
Te exorcizo!
Take your tricks and your wild ways
back to Andalusia.

Go home, poltergeist,
and do Spanish damage.
I have my own bad guests
that speak my own bad language.

WILLIAM GIRALDI
Hold the Dark

The wolves came down from the hills and carried away the children of Chinook. The village lay wedged into a horseshoe beneath those white hills, twelve winding miles from Norton Sound. First one child was taken at the start of winter as he tugged his sled at the edge of a slope; another was snatched the following week as she skirted the homes near the frozen pond. Now, in the rolling snow squalls of midwinter, a total of three children had been taken from the village, one from his own doorstep. Silently: no screams, no howls. The women were frantic, those who had lost their children inconsolable.

Many of the men of Chinook had gone overseas to fight in the war; it had been more than a year and still they were not back. The men who remained fished the gelid coastal waters of the Bering Sea for weeks at a time; others toiled in the mines for what little gold was left to salvage. They were of no help; the mourning wives were not theirs. On days off, some patrolled the borders of the village with rifles, some escorted children home from the schoolhouse or the church, but they would not send a party into the hills to hunt the wolves. It was clear that most saw the invading animals as punishment or retribution for some unnamed, nebulous sin. Police came thirty miles from the city of Nome one afternoon; they scratched down notes and did not return. The women, too, took up rifles, and cursed the men of their village: "If they were any good they'd be at the war."

Barbara Ranick's three-year-old son was the last to be taken. She told her neighbors how she had trekked over the hills all that evening and into the dawn with a Remington bolt action across her back and a ten-inch bowie on her right thigh. The wolves' tracks became scattered and then vague in the newly fallen snow. She dropped to her knees several times and watched her tears turn to ice. In her letter to Russell Curran just two days after the boy disappeared, she wrote that she did not expect to find him alive—a dotted trail of the boy's blood had led from their back porch and through the patchy iced woods into the hills above—but she needed his body, or what was left of it, if only bones. That's the reason she was writing Curran, she said, because she needed him to get her boy's bones and maybe slaughter the wolf that took him. "My husband is due back from the war in five months," she wrote, "and I must have something to show him. I need Ryan's bones for him. I can't have nothing." Curran would see that the torn-out notebook pages were not marked with tears.

He had retired from the U.S. Fish and Wildlife Service several years earlier and wrote an illustrated book on the timber wolf, an encyclopedic tome that took in four decades of studying the animal. The book included the dissertation for his doctorate, an investigation into the timber wolf's mating rituals—a dissertation written in an alien era, so long ago Curran scarcely believed in its reality. For the preface, he offered an essay on the only known wolf attack on a human in Yellowstone. A male timber crept into a campsite and stole an infant girl while the parents slept off their champagne. Curran explained this unparalleled incident as the result of food shortages, a late-arriving winter, and reckless human invasion into their domain: the roads, the campsites, the plastic trash, the oil-thirsty engines, all of it a massive affront to the majesty of what was there first.

Still, that day Curran tracked the wolf across twenty square miles over the Northern Range, through the Lamar Valley, and into Montana where he shot it from almost fifty yards on a cattle farmer's ranch. Through the scope he could see the wolf's white muzzle still sprayed pink with the child's raw innards, and pieces of yellow pajamas glued into the dried purple blood around its mouth. Examiners found most of the mashed girl inside the digestive track. "A murderer," the dead child's parents said of the wolf that robbed her. "A devil." But Curran knew this was not right. He wanted to scold them, hand them a summons for camping in a restricted valley, but did not.

Then he watched as, over the next ten years, the timber wolf was hunted to near extinction by cowards sniping from copters—deus ex machina—and he recoiled each time he remembered pulling the trigger on that adult male with the yellow strands of cloth stuck to its mouth. He became an active supporter of Yellowstone Reintroduction and penned newspaper editorials about the awful hubris. In her letter, Barbara Ranick wrote of Curran's book: "You're sympathetic to this animal. Please don't be. Come and kill it in the name of what's right. My son's bones are in the snow."

Curran had Barbara Ranick's letter folded into the pocket of his denim jacket when he arrived at the hospital in St. Paul. His wife of forty-two years lay where she had been for the past thirteen months, vegetative in a bed after a sudden stroke ripped through her like a zag of lightning. He wondered who was in charge, who held the strings. Curran did not sit. He stood looking at the complicated machines and computers at the side of her bed, the hoses and wires attached to her as if she were a faulty car battery that needed an extra jolt.

In the mirror above the sink, Curran saw his white mane spilling out from beneath a John Deere cap, the dense white whiskers sprouting from his face, a jaw that seemed elongated, and he wondered when he had gone so wintery, so irrevocably wolfish. Thirteen months ago, perhaps. Countless microwave dinners, the strange sleep of the sick, innumerable hours of quiet, the wind an almost welcome guest for the wail it made. How many more paintings could he produce of the wolf he had slain? The walls of his office and library were already hidden by his creations, always of the same wolf, always the yellow strands of cloth pasted into the hinge of its mouth.

Through the cotton blanket, he felt his wife's foot and grasped it gently in an uncertain gesture of goodbye. Was there a speech he was supposed to make now? He picked up his duffel bag and went. In the circular drive of the hospital's entrance sat waiting the same taxi that had delivered him.

Barbara Ranick wedged open her husband's letter with a finger—timidly, as if he had written to tell her news she already knew. She read it sitting at the edge of her son's bed—in a lane of weak sunlight, in spring's cruel tease—and what she read failed to haunt her, failed even to register.

Outside the city, the strong wind swept up sand, and when gusts passed before the low orange sun, they looked like blots of insects sent to swarm. Their vehicle preceded plumes of yellow dust; it trailed a rusted-through pickup truck packed with men. Perched at the .50 caliber gun, Ranick felt the sand pepper his face mask. This late in the day the temperature stayed fixed at over one hundred. Back home he knew it was snowing; another Alaskan winter he would not see. Behind him the city smoldered; if he pivoted he could behold the flames and smoke of this new Gomorrah. But before him he could see the wind-swept sand and the twirling dust of the truck perhaps fifty yards ahead. No one was shooting now; no one could see. Every few seconds, between the horizontal gusts, Ranick spotted the truck's tailgate. He squatted and shouted to his corporal, "Left. They're going left. Watch that decline."

Ranick saw the fleeing truck catch the gulley and overturn several times, silently, in a storm of sand and dust. He had seen trucks and snow machines flip in dense snow the same way: no sound. The men—what faction were they from? what region?—were flung from the truck's bed like wilted playthings. The truck crushed to a halt on top of them. Some limped from the tinfoil wreckage and shot at Ranick's vehicle: the lead dinged uselessly against the armor. When the .50 caliber rounds hit them they tore off limbs or left dark blue holes the size of fruit. Ranick fired into those on the petrol-soaked sand and those wedged inside the truck's flattened cab. Their blood burst in the wind as wisps of wet pink.

After minutes of no movement—he could almost behold the sun slinking down by inches to die for the day—he and his corporal approached the overturned truck. The boy inside was Ryan's age, beautiful new skin like the shine of caramel. Shoeless, his feet singed and melted and remolded: feet made from candle wax. The purple wound in his throat looked as if a clawed ogre had swiped at him in anger, the jugular ripped unevenly by glass or metal. He looked above him, around him, into the clueless eyes of his corporal. Who is in charge here? What foul game's pieces are we? Ranick waited until later to weep.

I'll be home in five months, he wrote his wife. *Tell our son five months is a flash.*

Curran landed in Alaska minutes before dark and rented a 4x4 truck to drive the one hundred miles to Chinook. The frozen landscape lay undulating but unseen beyond the green glow of the dashboard. Somber voices on the radio debated the war and the possibilities for ending it. The red and white pinpricks of light that passed across the sunroof were either planes or spaceships; Curran felt the possibility of a close encounter, of gunmetal trolls from a far-flung star descending to inquire about the likelihood of God. What would he tell them? And what would he tell Barbara Ranick about the wolf that filched her child? He realized that he had forgotten his blood pressure medication on the bathroom vanity...that he hadn't spoken to his daughter in almost three years now. An actress in Los Angeles. Soap operas, commercials Curran had never seen. Three slow years. Life was not short, as people insisted on saying. Life, he knew, took forever.

Barbara Ranick had tea ready when he finally arrived tired and unsettled. Curran was surprised by her youth; the woolen garb and disheveled hair of the grief-eaten were what he had expected, but her face did not fit: the face of a teenage softball player, not a woman with a dead boy and a husband off at war. Her cabin on the rim of the village was some builder's log mockery of a home, barely ample room to maneuver elbows and knees, a kitchenette squeezed into a corner, the stovepipe nearly vertical on the far wall like the black fossilized spine of an extinct behemoth. Curran could brush the ceiling with a fingertip. He noticed his book partially stuffed between two cushions of the sofa, the corners of pages folded over and under.

They sat across from each other—she on the sofa, he in the armchair—and sipped their tea. She offered him the refrigerated food that others from the village had been bringing to her since her son's disappearance—soup, bread, pie—but Curran had no appetite now. The tea warmed his body, a lone orange coal pulsating from somewhere in the center of his sternum.

"An apex predator," she said, moving his book to the coffee table between them. "An ice-age survivor from the Late Pleistocene. What's that mean?"

"It means they've been around a long time and know how to hunt better than most."

"You sound charmed."

"I'm sorry about your son, Mrs. Ranick. No mother should have to endure this."

"You've come to kill it? To kill the thing that stole him?"

"I'll kill it," he said. "If I can. But the boy's bones..."

"I was thinking that his bones would show during breakup, after the thaw."

"Breakup?"

"Spring."

Curran nodded; he did not tell her that this was impossible. The boy's yellow rubber boots stood on the welcome mat near the door, his navy pillowed coat on a hook, but there was no framed school photo grinning gap-toothed from the mantle, no plastic toys lying about. If not for the boots and coat, this woman before him would be just another forlorn story among many.

She said, "I would have killed the thing myself if I could have."

"Their territory could be up to seventy-five square miles. It's good you didn't find it. The pack is probably eight or ten members. No more than twelve. You don't want to find that."

"Do you have a child?"

"A daughter. She's grown now."

She looked into the steam of her mug but did not drink. "I don't understand what they're doing here," she said.

"Who?"

"Wolves."

"They've been here for half a million years, Mrs. Ranick. They walked over the Bering land bridge. They live here."

"I don't understand what they're doing *here*," and she gestured feebly in front of her, at the very space on the woven rug where her son had probably pieced together a puzzle of the solar system—or of nebulas, of supernovas, all that unfamiliar color captured by Hubble—or scribbled a drawing of the very animal that would one day come for him, stick-figure mommy and daddy looking on.

"Why is this happening to me, Mr. Curran? I can't stop it. What power is this?"

"Does your husband know about Ryan?"

"I can't tell him while he's there. He'll see for himself."

Curran nodded. "I think they're hungry and desperate. They don't leave for the fringes of their territory unless they're desperate. They avoid contact with humans if they can. If we'll let them."

He looked beyond her, looked for the proper vocabulary for this. "The caribou must have left early," he said. "For some reason."

He paused again. And then: "I don't know why this is happening to you, Mrs. Ranick."

He could have told her more, that a healthy gray wolf's yearly requirement of meat can reach two tons, that they'll eat each other if need be. A three-year-old boy would have shredded like tissue in the jaws of an adult male.

His tea was finished now and he felt the first shadows of sleep drop across him. Somewhere in the village, sled dogs barked up at constellations; both Curran and Barbara Ranick turned to look at the iced-black window. Where were the sled dogs when the wolves came? He recalled a Russian proverb: Do not call the dogs to help you against the wolves.

After a time, he said: "In Russia, during a winter of the Second World War, a food shortage was on. No meat, no grain. The fighting decimated the land. The wolves rampaged into villages and mauled almost at random. Like they were their own invading army. They killed hundreds of people that winter, and not just women and children. Drunk men or crippled men too weak to defend themselves. Even dogs. They left scenes of carnage almost as bad as the bombs. Blood in the streets. Doctors said they were rabid, but the villagers said they were possessed by demons hell-bent on revenge. Their howls, they said, sounded like hurt demons."

She stared at him; she didn't understand.

"You're not alone," he said. "For what it's worth."

"This war is never finished. What's done cannot be undone. Look what we're capable of, Mr. Curran," and she held up her hand just then to show him her palm. What would a soothsayer predict about her coming life from the crisscrossed lines on that palm? She looked to Curran like a woman with only yesterdays.

And he could have told her stories about war too, if she wanted to know. About how he had witnessed two rival packs of wolves ruin each other in the Lamar Valley, each pack its own phalanx, one slamming into the other in a forty-mile-per-hour sprint of calculation or madness, their tails raised stiff, lips curled back, incisors gleaming, those paws with bristled hair and blunted claws stuck on snow like the knobbed tread of trucks. Amazing evolution: modified capillaries in their paws that prevent frostbite. Masterpieces of stamina. And through the warring howls, Curran imagined the deafening clang of armor on armor, sword on shield, the heaves of human beings as breath left their bodies and mingled with smoke. To someone who referred to wolves as merely glorified canines—no better than suburban dogs gone after balls—Curran only smirked. No, they weren't dogs. A brain one-third larger, a jaw so forceful it delivers twice the pressure of the strongest dog. And war. Always war. That clamor in the Lamar Valley.

She said, "I want to show you where the children were taken," and Curran had to lift himself from the chair.

The village was enclosed in snow and silence. Orange windows burned in the sides of homes; white smoke surged from chimneys. Curran saw dog sleds, wood piles, trucks with chains on the tires. Shovels and snow machines. And all around, the hills that threatened to close like a fist.

"It's a beautiful place," he told her, his white breath heavy before his face.

"My husband left me alone in this beautiful place." She neither tensed against the cold nor appeared to feel the chill on her naked hands.

"But the war," he said.

"He volunteered. That means he didn't have to go, to leave me with a sick child."

"Some men have to go."

"That's the pond where the first was taken," and she pointed.

"Your son was sick?"

"Sick, slow, whatever you call it. Couldn't go to school. Cried day and night. Cried and cried deranged." She pointed again. "The wolf came from that dip in the hill, beyond the far side of the water."

Curran saw the snow-covered rectangular mound he guessed was a dock. Children leapt from that dock in summer, but imagining the sounds of their splashes was not possible now.

"The second was taken over here," she said, and they walked around the pond, behind a row of cabins to where the low front hills split and formed an icy alcove. "The children sled in here, down that hill there."

"Ryan too?"

"Ryan didn't sled."

They stood staring into the alcove as if trying to imagine the wolf charging down from the slope and dragging away a startled child. A wind lifted from the east and carried white blurs of snow. Curran knew he should have felt the hollowed eeriness of examining a crime scene, except that his travel had blunted everything but exhaustion.

"How did it feel to shoot that wolf?" she asked.

"We don't have a choice in some matters, Mrs. Ranick."

She said, "I suppose you're hungry now. I have soup."

When they arrived at the Ranicks' front door, Curran said, "Where was Ryan taken?"

"Around back," she said, and gestured with her chin at the corner of the cabin.

"May I see?"

"I'd rather you didn't."

Barbara Ranick heated a dented pot of soup on the burner. In the armchair, Curran ate from the pot and allowed the broth to transform him, to abolish any last remnants of his ability to fend off sleep.

She said, "I left a quilt and pillow here for you, Mr. Curran." She rose from the sofa and placed her mug on the countertop. "Thank you for coming here. I can't pay you anything."

"It's all right," he said, and Barbara Ranick turned the corner into her bedroom.

He heard her say, "To bed, to bed," and the door clicked shut.

Before Curran let sleep drag him down into darkness, the howl of a wolf came clear and mournful through the snow-dense night. The male timber he had tracked into Montana so long ago howled at him—he knew it was at him—from across five to eight miles of mostly flat expanse. It howled as if it knew Curran was coming—howled in reproach, in expression of what nature had made it. Many nights, Curran expected to be jarred awake by dreams of that wolf, by the sharp crack of the rifle round, and when he slept soundly through till the dawn, he woke feeling guilty that his slumber had not been disrupted.

With sleep coming on now, just milliseconds away, Curran thought he heard the mutters of Barbara Ranick from her bedroom, Christian prayers or else the incantations of a witch, whispered songs through sobs, impossible entreaties of the dispossessed. And then sometime in the center of his sleep Curran woke to the distinct naked figure of Barbara Ranick silhouetted before the picture window, standing motionless with her hand on the glass, the blue-white night unnaturally intense around her. The folds of her waist, heavy breasts falling to either side of her ribcage, the tiny cup of flesh from her elbow: Curran lay in fear looking at her over the length of his cosseted body, his breath stifled lest she hear him, lest he disrupt this midnight vigil, this beckoning of frozen ghosts.

"Is he up there?" she asked after several minutes. Her voice, no more than a murmur, came to him as if from across an empty chamber.

"It's late, Mrs. Ranick. Are you all right?"

She turned to peer at him lying on the sofa. If he sat up, he could reach over the cushioned arm and stroke her hip, her breast, no more than a yard away. When she moved toward him, he instinctively peeled the quilt and turned his body to make room. She fit into him imperfectly, the sofa sank, and he covered them in the quilt. With her back to him, she took his hand and brought it to her throat, folding it around her windpipe, trying to will his grip to squeeze. Curran recovered his hand and draped his arms around her and held her still flesh until she passed into sleep. All the while he inhaled her shampooed hair and tried to recall the long-forgotten girl the scent reminded him of: not his wife in youth, not his daughter as a teen, but a girl long before them, a girl he was certain now he must have loved.

Barbara Ranick watched Curran leave at dawn with the AR-15 semi-automatic rifle and a backpack of provisions and snowshoes. The call came shortly after, and she thought, *The call always comes.* Matthew Ranick's voice streamed through the line so crisply it was as if he were there before her in his sweat-marked fatigues, sand in the crevices of his equipment. But in the middle of the story he told, his voice seemed to shrivel into static as Barbara Ranick looked unblinkingly at her bare feet and the lines in the wood beneath them.

On patrol through the eastern sector of the city in the midday swelter, he saw pyramids of tires flaming on street corners, the buildings reduced to irregular mounds of rubble. Their vehicle crawled and stopped and crawled again, not knowing where it wanted to be, uncertain of motion's mandates. First his yawns from an ugly, dream-plagued sleep the night before, his wishes of being in a snow-covered landscape, the questions of purpose that come from decay. And then his unclear vision from the fires, black smoke like a poisoned cloud eager to stifle. And then the rapid snaps from rifles on a rooftop or from a gaping, jagged hole in the façade of a structure. Matthew Ranick knew that one round had entered his right deltoid; he could feel the blood, the heated honey in his armpit. He scattered the .50 caliber rounds into the bricks of a building, into doors, into a disabled Toyota with a missing front axle. The explosion in his neck felt like the release of steam or gas, and when he slumped down onto the vehicle expecting blackness, he thought of Ryan in front of the television: *Dad, look at this, look,* and on the screen were trapeze artists breaking free of gravity, soaring, immortal. Sometime later—he couldn't tell how long— he woke on a gurney carried by his men, his corporal grinning, saying, "You lucky son of a bitch, you're going home." The small caliber round had gone in and out without passing through vital pieces. "Nothing but a hickey, Matt," someone said, and in another minute sleep lowered him into a grateful dark where he dreamed of Icarus attached to wings not of wax but of reinforced steel.

I'll be home in just a few days, he told his wife, and when the phone call was finished, Barbara Ranick sat on the sofa and stared at the air in front of her, as if trying to understand how oxygen enters a body and keeps the brain alive. In hemoglobin. Plasma. White and red cells. Blue inside, crimson out. *A body for a body and many more.*

The flakes came down the size of quarters, and Curran saw the beginning of gray daylight through the trees to the east. At the perimeter of the village, near the base of the hill where the path led up and around, Curran came upon an old back-bent Inuit woman burning things in a rusted steel drum. He glimpsed her through the spider-webbed assemblage of limbs and twigs groping from dead trees. He stopped on the path to see if she would notice him, and when she did, she waved him over to the fire. Curran saw the red-orange radiance on her tanned face, her winter garb thick and soiled, but could not tell what blazed in the drum. He guessed she was burning trash.

She said, "I thought you were something wicked."

"No, ma'am," he said. "I'm heading into the hills."

She cackled. "To get a wolf's tooth, I've been told."

"Yes," he said. "How do you know?"

"We're a small village. We've had enough toil and trouble here."

He said, "The wolves. I know. I'm sorry."

"You don't know. You think you do."

What house in the village was hers? What compelled her out here before dawn? Curran could not ask.

She said, "You would bar the door against the wolf, why not more against beasts with the souls of damned men, against men who would damn themselves to beasts?"

"I'm sorry?"

"*We* are sorry."

The flame widened in the barrel and Curran could feel its heat. "I'll get on now," he said, and made to move up the path. "Have a good day."

"You're going the wrong way," she said, not turning her face from the heated glow of the drum. "Go back the way you came," and she pointed a crooked finger to the snowed-over main road of the village.

Curran ignored her and continued up the path.

He expected to find a pack in the shallow valley on the other side of these hills, a den tucked away on a rocky ridge. He knew the boy's bones would not be in the den; it had been ten days since his death and his skeleton was no doubt spread through the wilderness by scavengers, covered by virgin snowfall. There would be no burial, no coming to terms. But he would kill a wolf if he could and cart it back for the woman, tell her it was the monster that seized her son. Perhaps she'd be able to quit the midnight vigils and sleep through till first light knowing that a killer had been removed from the world. Perhaps not. Curran slogged on through the thick snow, the sack of food and ammunition hanging heavy on his shoulders, heavier than normal.

The Apache hunted timber wolves as a rite of passage; a wolf-kill turned an adolescent into a leader. And now Curran was hunting one for a reason and a woman he did not know.

Two hours into his trek he stopped beneath a rock face on the far side of the hills. The snowfall had ceased and the sun blinked on and off behind ice clouds. While eating an egg and bacon sandwich Barbara Ranick had wrapped for him—still warm in the foil—he heard the first howls down in the valley, forty yards away over the tallest crest in the hills. He had seen no caribou tracks; no coyotes. What pestilence was on this land? On the crest of the hill, he peered down into the valley and spotted a pack against the facing ridge, a frenzy of ten gray wolves. Through the field glasses Curran could see an infant wolf or coyote in the center of the frenzy, several jaws clamped into its flesh, the adult wolves tugging, angling for leverage, the bounty shorn in a mess of purple and pink. Ambling down the slope, Curran lost footing in the snow and slid several yards until his snowshoes stopped against a boulder. He sidestepped the rest of the way until he met the iced plain. There he sat and watched through the glasses as the maw of wolves consumed the last of the carcass.

After checking to make certain that the rifle's magazine was full, Curran loaded the first round into the gun's chamber and set off slowly across the plain, the surface hoar crunching beneath his feet. As the plain undulated, only slightly, Curran lost sight of the wolves, but he knew that as soon as the wind shifted west his scent would reach them. They would attempt as a team to dismantle him; he had witnessed them prey on bison and caribou, a pack of four gray wolves defeating a one-ton beast with a pelt like iron. This was what he wanted, he guessed. Dismantling. A body for a body.

Soon Curran topped the last small crest in the plain and the pack knew he was there. From a quarter mile distant, the wolves began their charge, half head-on and half on each flank. They'd surround him, he knew, and he dropped to one knee and stayed in wait with the rifle pointed at the alpha out front, a male maybe six years old, a hundred and fifty pounds. The white dust of trampled snow lifted among the pack and glittered in the frames of sunlight. Was this the wolf that took the children of Chinook, this deep silver male with a faultless stride coming at Curran now with no thought, no malice, no want other than what its ancient blood propelled it to do? Curran centered the wolf's skull in the crosshairs of the rifle's scope; in half a minute or less the pack would be on him, the alpha tearing at his throat, the others at his limbs. His breathing came slow and even, his heart-rate quickened by only a beat. He imagined slow motion and no sound; he knew they must be ravenous to charge him like this, only days away from starvation, from disappearance.

When, at the last instant, he fired at the air above the leader's skull, the pack halted at the echoed crack of the round and glanced at each other in puzzlement or displeasure. When they neither advanced nor retreated, another shot at the clouds scattered them westward from where they came along the ridge at the far side of the valley. Curran would tell the woman that the wolves were gone, remind her that what was done could not be undone, that blood does not remove blood. He had half-expected to perish out here this morning, to freeze and be lost, or else be ravaged by wolves and dispersed into everything. Some of him had wanted this. Most of him hadn't.

Curran trekked through the afternoon, resting for long stretches, and when he arrived back at Barbara Ranick's house, the early dying of the day had begun. She did not answer his knock on the wood frame. When he entered he saw her bedroom door thrown open, clothes oozing out of the closet and strewn along the carpet, a suitcase with a broken handle lying on its side like a dropped wallet. He called her name but she did not answer. The cold still infused his face; fatigue moved through his thighs; and the hole in his center felt forged by a force greater than hunger, older than longing.

Weak light knifed through from beneath the narrow door that, the night before, Curran had thought was a closet. When he opened it, a chill hastened up from the basement and swept his skin. The rounded steps had been made from available rock, the sharply slanted ceiling so low he had to crouch to clear his head, a stairwell designed for dwarves. A bare lightbulb illuminated this cramped space, little more than a cubbyhole, one half of the foundation made not from cinder block but from local stone. The Ranicks had nothing stored here: no cardboard boxes of junk, no Christmas decorations awaiting the season. Curran's breath, opaque and white, hung before him as he moved beneath the light. Stones had been dislodged from the wall behind the steps; a nook had been dug into the permafrost. The light did not reach here; shadows fell with weight, with purpose. Curran removed a glove to strike a match. He moved nearer. Inside the hole, the frozen body of a boy leaned against the earth, cocooned in cellophane, his open eyes iced over and stuck skyward.

Curran would rest here now for some time, sitting slumped in the corner on an overturned bucket, wondering about the opposite of miracles, remembering his hand around the throat of Barbara Ranick, how she beckoned retribution. His daughter had made her new life in Los Angeles. How far south was she from him? How to reach her through this ice? Soon Curran would rise, walk through the village on trembling legs, knock on doors, shout down roads. He would not know that at the other end of the earth, in an arid wasteland, a wounded soldier was prepared to board a transport plane, prepared to trade sand for snow, unprepared for the wish of reversal. Nor would Curran see the old Inuit woman at the base of the hill burning photographs in a barrel, pictures of the children from this village, in the hope that their faces would arrive in smoke before the eyes of winter gods, and that these gods would protect them from harm.

SYDNEY LEA
Not Like Adamo

> *I have had just about all I can take of myself.*
> —S. N. Behrman

There's a rose bush outside, like the one by the kitchen
where Serena some evenings uncovered a pasta dish,
beyond exquisite.
My new wife and I would inhale its perfumes and sigh.
Not like Adamo, her husband, who'd barely touch it.

I won't play retrospection's fool
like him as he dawdled, lachrymose, in his chair,
old alleys traced
by worms along its chestnut grain now showing
patterns. Lovely. Serpentine. Complex.

We stayed near Florence in that long gone summer…
Enough! as Adamo would surely not have said.
Enough! *Basta!*
In older age I tire of memory,
don't want it to be, like his, my liveliest asset,

to call it so, for what's left of my life.
I can pledge at least henceforth that I'll offer fewer
of my rote recursions—
to the limestone arch in their tiny village, for instance,
and how one day it framed my beautiful woman;

how a pair of doves, each white as flax,
sped out at me, and in their flight passed close
above her shoulders;
how a fountain winked. Enchantment. Archaic poets

would have styled the sky *empyrean,* I'd venture…

To hell with habitual reminiscence.
I'm thinking right now instead of one of my sons.
He builds guitars.
Where does it come from, his preternatural deftness?
The instruments are no doubt works of art,

to his father akin to those magical paintings
by Fra Angelico we saw in San Marco,
from which we stepped out,
my love and I, into sun and other enchantment:
a small *gelateria,* where no doubt

she was beautiful too, and the ice cream's flavor
of lemon so true…That son himself has children.
So does one of his sisters.
Our clan's alive. No reason to elegize
the vanished infancies of sons and daughters,

though once I held all five as babies,
their warming breaths on my neck…Why spend my strength,
why wrack my head
like Adamo, who squandered years in invocation
of his offspring's juvenescence—and in mourning his dead?

January's whiteout weather
hails the death of a year, the stocks of the rose
outside turned wan
as phantoms while—to think of things more freshly—
a different, younger year struts boldly in.

ANNA MARGOLIN
The Years

Translated from the Yiddish by Maia Evrona

Like women who are loved to the fullest and are still unsatisfied,
and go through life with laughter and with rage
in their eyes of fire and agate—
so were the years.

And they also appeared to be as actors,
hesitantly performing *Hamlet* before the market;
as grandiose landowners in a proud land,
who will seize an uprising by its throat.

And see, my God, how meek they are now,
and dumb as a smashed piano,
and they take for love every impulse and ridicule,
and search for you, not believing in you.

JENNIFER HAIGH

Paramour

The tribute was held downtown, far away from the theater district. Christine crossed the street gingerly, on four-inch heels thin as pencils—Ivan had always loved women in high heels—and checked the address against the invitation in her purse. The building was new and modern, the front window lettered with Cyrillic characters and a boldface translation: **UKRAINIAN CULTURAL CENTER**. She'd forgotten, nearly, that he was born in that country. To her he'd been a New Yorker, nothing else.

The upstairs gallery was large, the wood floors gleaming. A hundred chairs were arranged in a horseshoe, facing an improvised stage. At the door, a girl handed out programs—shyly, as if embarrassed by her unflattering but perhaps authentically Ukrainian hairstyle, a long braid wrapped around her head.

In the front row—**RESERVED FOR BORYSENKO FAMILY AND FRIENDS**—a woman sat alone. Christine studied her plump shoulders, her blond hair twisted into a loose chignon. *Beth,* she thought. The wife's name was lodged in her memory like a bullet that could not be removed. Ivan's marriage, its happiness or unhappiness, had once consumed her completely. On his desk, he'd kept a single photograph: the mysterious Beth sitting nude, her back to the camera; a naked infant asleep on her shoulder; a wash of pale hair hanging down her back. Now she wore a batiked sundress. Her cleavage was deep and freckled, skin that had spent forty or fifty summers in the sun.

The room filled, hummed, quieted. A half dozen men took seats on the stage. Finally Ivan came striding down the aisle with a girl on his arm. The crowd burst into applause.

He'd aged, of course. His hair, still longish and wavy, was now more gray than black. He whispered something to the girl—a round-faced brunette, impossibly young, squeezed into a clinging dress.

"Let me guess. You were his favorite student."

Christine turned, startled by the intimacy. The man had leaned in close to her ear. For a second she'd felt his breath on her neck.

"I'm Martin, by the way." He was her own age, handsome like a pirate—shaved head, a deeply suntanned face.

"Christine. How did you know I was his student?"

"Ivan is nothing if not consistent." The man spoke in an unfamiliar accent. "He's always had an eye for blondes."

Christine glanced at the front row, where Ivan and the girl sat shoulder to shoulder. "It seems his tastes have changed."

Martin followed her gaze.

"Darling, that's Pia," he said. "Ivan's daughter."

Ivan Borysenko had been her teacher, a visiting professor at the small, good upstate college she'd attended on scholarship. He'd come from the city on a one-year appointment to teach playwriting, a subject that hadn't interested her in the slightest until he appeared.

She'd been a mercurial student, prone to infatuations: philosophy to French lit, Rousseau and Voltaire to Sartre and Genet. She'd studied these subjects with roughly equal aptitude, a generalist excelling at nothing, until Ivan came along.

He pronounced his name distinctly, with a soft roll of the R. *Borrysenko.* "It's Ukrainian," he explained, to blank stares. The Soviet Union had not yet crumbled; American students were unaware, still, of the many countries it comprised: the multitude of languages, plosive and sibilant; the lumbering syllables of those impenetrable names.

Christine's first effort, a surrealistic one-act, had piqued his interest—and Ivan's interest, she learned, was an irresistible force. She felt caught by him, mounted like a butterfly, held fast for his consideration and delight. Her nineteen-year-old self appeared to fascinate him completely, Christine who had never fascinated anybody in her life. He selected her play for a student production, and taught her to run auditions and rehearsals. They were assumed to be lovers, a misconception she didn't correct. She was not, strictly speaking, a virgin. With her best friend, a boy named Tommy, she had suffered two attempts—one failed, one nominally successful; both awkward and crushingly sad. In the end, Tommy dropped out of school to be the lover of a wealthy man, surprising no one but Christine, who would love him the rest of his days. That he had loved but not desired her was a truth she confided to no one. She carried the shame like a disfiguring scar.

Ivan's attentions, in private, were fierce and febrile; but it was his public devotion that thrilled her. As they crossed the campus together, she felt lit up from inside. This handsome older man, brilliant and sophisticated, had chosen Christine Mooney, wanted and had her: this belief was etched on her classmates' faces. To Christine, at nineteen, it was more than enough.

The tribute lasted two hours, glowing testimonials by writers and directors, a charismatic Irish actor she'd seen, a lifetime ago, on stage. They spoke of Ivan's lasting imprint on the New York theater, the generations of students he'd molded and shaped. His twenty-year marriage to Beth, his rock and muse; his famous devotion to Pia, who was born remarkable and became more extraordinary—it was agreed—with each passing year.

In the front row, Ivan sat between them, an arm around each.

After the final applause, the standing ovation, he was caught in a scrum of well-wishers. "He'll be stuck here for an hour," Martin predicted, guiding Christine through the crowd, his hand hovering lightly at her back.

She and Martin shared a cab to Paramour, the Soho restaurant where the afterparty would be held. "South African," Martin said when she asked about his accent. He was a dramaturge at Circle Rep, a job Ivan had helped him secure. Christine nodded and smiled, asked pertinent questions, and barely registered his answers, her mind elsewhere.

Paramour was already crowded, samba music nearly lost in the conversational roar. Christine stood in a corner waiting for Martin to bring their drinks. Waiters circulated precariously with trays of appetizers. All around her, strangers stood back to back, elbow to elbow—New Yorkers accustomed to crowds, to chaos. Old friends shrieked greetings; acquaintances made small talk at the top of their lungs. No one seemed to find this unsettling or strange.

She recognized a few faces from the tribute. At the bar, two playwrights shouted past each other. Across the room, Ivan's daughter told a story to a rapt audience. The evening's speeches had established that Pia was used to the spotlight. (At four she'd sat for a renowned Polish photographer, a portrait now hanging in the Guggenheim. She'd inspired a series of children's books written by a friend of Ivan's, and by her tenth birthday was eligible for an Equity card.) Christine watched her keenly, an ordinary-looking teenage girl, flushed and happy, tugging occasionally at her slinky dress. Her audience—a well-dressed couple, the Irish actor, a woman in a fedora—seemed captivated, their eyes bright and encouraging, as though watching a baby's first steps. In Christine's family, children were not lavished with such attention. Her mother would have called Pia a show-off. Christine found her marvelous.

She glanced out at the patio. A gray-haired man in Armani stood smoking, talking into a headset clipped to his ear. He stopped speaking when a pretty boy asked him for a light. The boy was blond and very young. He wore a silky shirt, blue paisley, that lay like paint on his skin.

I could never live anywhere else, Ivan had often said. To Christine, at nineteen, New York had seemed not merely the height of civilization but its actual center, the most vital point on earth. Later—after Tommy's illness, his slow wasting—the city became a cemetery, a vast and teeming grave. His final month had been spent in a downtown hospice. His wealthy lover had paid for his care, but it was Christine who'd slept in a chair by his bed.

A kiss landed on her bare shoulder, Martin returning with their drinks. "Bold, I know. I would have tapped your shoulder, but my hands are full." He handed her a wineglass. "No sign of the great man?"

"Not yet." Outside, the man and the boy leaned against the brick wall, their faces hidden in shadow. They tossed away their cigarettes and lit two more. This time the boy leaned in close, holding the man's hand to steady the flame.

Martin waved to someone in the distance. "Everyone bores me," he said. "Tell me about you and Ivan."

Christine colored. "I haven't seen him in fifteen years. I have no idea why I'm here." Astonishingly, the invitation had arrived in the mail. She'd moved a half dozen times since college—to France on a Fulbright, to grad school, back to France. She'd touched down briefly in Chicago for a visiting professorship. Now, once again, her possessions were crossing the country in a moving van.

"My own parents can't keep track of me," she said. "I can't imagine where he got my address."

Martin frowned. "Beth didn't invite you?"

"I've never met her in my life." Again Christine glanced out the window. The man and the boy had disappeared. She felt a flash of disappointment and then, a sudden jolt. Ivan was crossing the patio—alone, his hands in his pockets, as though she'd conjured him from the air.

The room seemed suddenly quiet.

"Excuse me," she whispered, and pushed her way through the crowd.

She had never gone to bed with him. In truth, she hadn't considered it: his wedding ring, the wife and baby waiting for him in New York. What they'd done instead had seemed harmless—less serious, anyway, than *adultery*. There was still enough parochial school in her to make her blanch at the word.

Later she understood how gravely she'd miscalculated. That with every lover for the rest of her life, Ivan Borysenko would hover in the room.

She'd sat for him as a model sits for an artist. This was how he'd explained it the first time—a weeknight, late, after a long rehearsal. In his apartment, he'd watched intently as she took off her clothes. She hesitated over her bra and panties.

Everything, he said. I need to see it all.

Naked, she awaited further instruction. She lay sometimes on the floor of his apartment, sometimes the bed or the living-room couch. His bed was made, always, with crisp white sheets. She lay on her back, gazing up at him. He watched her for a long time, his eyes half closed, his arms crossed. When asked, she turned on her side or belly, raised her arms or opened her legs. He did not touch her, or himself.

"Thank you, my love," he would say finally, her signal to dress and disappear. To leave him alone with the fresh memory of her.

They sat together on the dark patio. "Tell me everything," Ivan said, "about your life."

Quickly she rattled off the details: the PhD in French lit, the Fulbright, her new tenure-track job in California.

He lit a cigarette. "It's a pity you stopped writing. I was sure you'd continue. You were a great talent."

Her face went hot with pleasure.

"I tried for a while," she admitted. "Then I gave up and went to grad school. It's OK," she added hastily. And then, not sure if it was true: "I'm happy."

"I'm not. It shocks me that you have defected from the theater."

It was a script she remembered from long ago: Ivan playing the wounded prima donna. Her role, now, was to placate him. "I haven't defected entirely," she said. "I teach Racine and Corneille."

He looked incredulous. "Your students are still interested in classicism? Even today?"

"I'm not sure how interested they are in literature, period."

"Literature is something one reads," he snapped. "Racine and Corneille never intended their work to be read."

He stared at her a long moment, the avid dark eyes she remembered. In the shadow of his apartment they'd seemed to be all pupil. "What became of your friend Tommy?" he asked. "He was a great talent."

Her smile faded. *A great talent.* The words, she realized, were meaningless, a stock phrase he used to flatter his former students. How many times would he say it this evening? That noisy room was filled, probably, with great talents.

"I don't know," she lied. "We lost touch years ago."

"Daddy!"

Christine turned. Pia was crossing the patio in their direction, a wineglass in her hand.

"Darling." Ivan rose. "Christine, I'd like you to meet my greatest creation. My daughter, Pia."

Pia offered her hand, moist from the glass. "Nice to see you." It was the neat phrase everyone used nowadays, to greet a stranger one perhaps ought to recognize but didn't quite recall. Christine marveled at her composure. She tried to imagine herself at seventeen, out late on a school night in such a dress, drinking wine in full view of her parents. Teenage Christine celebrated in public, praised and flattered, the shining object of adult attention. The image refused to materialize.

Her mind could not conceive of it.

Ivan kissed Pia's forehead. "It's eleven o'clock. You're going to turn into a pumpkin."

"Another hour," she said. "I'll be gone by midnight. Poof!"

"You won't miss a thing. The party will fizzle without you." His gaze was tender, his tone nearly flirtatious. Christine's stomach cramped violently, a wave of sickness. Jealousy was a bodily emotion. It lived in the entrails, a malevolent parasite.

They watched the girl walk away, teetering on high heels.

"She's taking the SATs in the morning," Ivan said. "She was supposed to leave at eleven."

"How will she get home?" It seemed necessary to feign interest, to partake in the general fascination with Pia. Though in fact she'd already heard more about Ivan's daughter—much, much more—than she wanted to know.

"Beth's parents bought her a car. Her boyfriend is the designated driver. He doesn't drink." Ivan pointed to a corner of the patio, where Pia was sharing a cigarette with the blond boy in the blue paisley shirt.

"Him?" Christine said.

(Possibly her perspective was skewed. Possibly—in New York, the memory of Tommy clutching her like a lonely ghost—she saw hustlers everywhere.)

"Where are you staying?" Ivan asked.

When she named the hotel, he nodded thoughtfully. "I'll meet you later. We can have a drink."

His dark eyes cut through her like a laser, as though he could see through her skin. Of course, it was the reason she had come: to be looked at in this way.

Her heart worked loudly inside her. "What about your wife?"

He shrugged elaborately, gracefully, like a dancer stretching.

"It was Beth who made the guest list. She knows I love surprises." He took her hand in both of his. "It's my night, after all. You're a present for me."

Inside, the air conditioning was going full force. Christine took a seat at the bar, shivering in the cold. She flagged a waiter passing with a tray of appetizers and took one of everything, a tiny quiche, a skewer of grilled chicken, a pile of tomatoes on toast. Eating, she thought back to the shadowy afternoons with Ivan, his bare off-campus apartment, the shades pulled to the sills, his hungry gaze clicking like a camera. After he sent her away, what had he done with the images in his head? She'd believed, always, that the pictures were for him alone. Now she imagined him calling his wife in the city. *The girl was here. She sat for me.*

Beth had known all along.

Christine, in her innocence, had never imagined such a thing: that her secret afternoons with Ivan were no secret, those burning hours that had marked her like a brand. That in actual fact she'd been part of his marriage, covered under the contract. Ivan loved women. His work took him to Los Angeles and London, to theaters and college campuses. His wife, pragmatic, had granted him certain freedoms. *Look, but don't touch.*

"There you are." Martin laid a hand on her shoulder. She felt herself leaning into it, the living heat of his hand.

"I saw you outside with Ivan. I considered joining you, but he would have torn me apart with his teeth. You're freezing," he said, rubbing her arm.

He took an olive from her plate.

"Alex Tinsley is here. His play is getting fabulous reviews. Have you seen it?"

"I haven't seen anything," she said.

"How refreshing. I'm sick to death of the theater." His eyes wandered. "Let me nab Tinsley before he leaves. Don't move. I don't want to lose you again."

She watched him cut through the crowd of great talents: actors performing at each other, directors thinking aloud, playwrights testing out speeches, auditioning their own words. Theater people were born to be looked at, though it occurred to Christine—not for the first time—that they were more impressive from a distance, observed from the mezzanine, the house lights dimmed. Their intricate private lives—Ivan's and Beth's, Tommy's—were best left in shadow. Only Racine and Corneille, dead three centuries, could be safely studied, their strange passions consigned to the past.

"Thank Jesus. A chair."

Christine turned. Pia sat heavily next to her and removed a shoe. "My feet are killing me. How do you walk in those?" She looked bleary, a little drunk, her makeup smeared.

"Never stand when you don't have to. Seriously. Try to spend the whole night sitting down." An errant bra strap slid down the girl's shoulder. Christine resisted the urge to adjust it, as her mother would have done.

"Have you seen Justin?"

A moment passed before she understood that Justin was the boyfriend. Famous since birth, Pia assumed—usually correctly—that everyone in her orbit knew the details of her life.

"He's supposed to drive me home? To Montclair? That looks so good. I'm off carbs." She eyed the toast on Christine's plate. "For this dress. I haven't had bread in a week."

"The night is over," Christine said, handing her the plate.

Pia took it, smiling gratefully. Her hands were plump as a toddler's. She ate the toast in two bites. Hungry baby, Christine thought, and wished she had more to feed her, an entire loaf of bread.

She watched Pia lurch away, teetering in her shoes, and thought, *Seventeen. That's what seventeen looks like.* She'd been just two years older, a college sophomore, when she sat for Pia's father.

By one o'clock the crowd had dwindled. Christine watched Ivan from across the room, ambushed again and again by well-wishers.

"I've had enough," she told Martin.

"Likewise," he said quickly, draining his glass. "Let's go."

For years afterward she'd wonder how the night might have unfolded if she'd simply gone back to her hotel to wait for Ivan. Would she have sat for him as she'd done before—still and silent, untouched and unloved? What, exactly, were the terms of Beth's gift?

Instead, in the taxi, she kissed Martin passionately. Let the ghosts hover: his body was a tangible thing, arms and hands and shoulders. His mouth felt warm and alive. *Yes to everything,* she thought. *Do everything to me.*

Later, lying awake in Martin's bed, she imagined Ivan appearing at her hotel in midtown, waiting as the front desk rang her room. She found out, later, that he'd turned off his cell phone and missed the call when it came. A New Jersey state trooper had found Pia's car on the Garden State Parkway, nosed into a concrete barrier, Pia unconscious behind the wheel. A generation ago, before airbags, she would have been thrown through the windshield. Instead the giant cushion rose up to receive her, holding her fast. Her injuries were not serious, but the SATs took place without her. She spent two days in a private hospital room filled with flowers. By day she entertained a constant stream of visitors. At night her father kept vigil beside her bed.

J. D. McCLATCHY
Prelude, Delay, and Epitaph

1.

A finger is cut from a rubber glove
And clamped as a tourniquet around my toe.
The gouging ingrown nail is to be removed.
The shots supposed to have pricked and burned
The nerves diabetes has numbed never notice.
The toe, as I watch, slowly turns a bluish
Gray, the color of flesh on a slab, the size
Of a fetus floating on the toilet's Styx,
But lumpen, the blunt hull of a tug slowly
Nosing the huge, clumsy vessel into port.

2.

The February
Moon, its arms around itself,
Still sits stalled beneath

Points being made about love
And death in the sky above.

The moral is spread
On some month-old snow out back—
A design we like

To think night can make of day,
The summons again delayed.

3.

You who read this too will die.
None loved his life as much as I,
Yet trees burst brightly into bloom
Without me, here in my darkened room.

ANN HOOD
Code Blue

Iris wants to walk on the beach with her feet in the ocean and the sun on her face. She wants to eat greasy hamburgers and drink pints of beer and throw peanut shells on the floor. She wants to wear high heels, polish the silver, dance the tango, bake a cake, plant peonies, daydream, sleep in a real bed, drink good coffee, waste time. Mostly, Iris wants her husband to die, finally, so she can leave this hospital and go home.

But he will not die. He clings to life stubbornly, futilely, relentlessly. The Energizer Bunny, the nurses say. Are they impressed? Or, like Iris, exhausted by Toby's will to live?

She stares at him: tubes in his nose, oxygen mask over mouth, IVs and catheters, all plastic tubing snaking out from beneath the sheets, a rainbow of liquids, some his (the yellow, the red), some theirs (the milky white and almost blue and buttercream).

Die, Iris thinks as she watches the slow but steady rise and fall of his chest. Reliable was how everyone used to describe Toby. He sold insurance, was fastidious with details, drove the speed limit, cleaned the gutters. An upright citizen. Only in this does he shake his fist at life and hang on. *Die already,* she thinks.

Their daughter Gwendolyn appears in the doorway with her salt-and-pepper hair in some kind of lopsided bun and wearing too much large vaguely ethnic jewelry. She teaches Film Studies at Brown, but she has never seen a movie that anyone else has seen.

"I've lost my keys," Gwendolyn says. She jangles into the room, her beads and bells and shells bumping angrily into each other. "Can't get in my apartment or my office, so I figured I'd keep you company."

Iris' day has just gotten worse.

"How is he?" Gwendolyn asks, pointing her chin toward her father.

"Still alive," Iris says.

Gwendolyn laughs; she is the only one of the three girls who would laugh at this. Mallory, the baby even at thirty-two, would cry and ask how Iris could say such a thing. Charlotte would nod solemnly and tell

Iris that she was in denial. But Gwen, intelligent, foolish, careless Gwen, can at least laugh at how ridiculous Toby's condition has become.

From her oversize woven bag—Guatemalan? Ecuadorian?—Gwendolyn pulls out a stack of papers to correct and gets right to it. Toby snorts and moans, and Iris holds her breath. But no, he takes another big deep breath. Then another.

Iris sighs and turns her attention to the Sudoku puzzle she is working on. Charlotte gave her an entire book of them to keep her busy. Sudoku is mind-numbingly dull, like second grade arithmetic. She studies her little boxes of numbers and sees she has two 9s in the same row. She erases one of them and thinks about a perfect Manhattan. Toby used to make the best Manhattans, with Maker's Mark, sweet and dry vermouth, bitters. He used to light the orange peel and let its oils infuse the cocktail.

"Coffee break!" Mallory tweets from the doorway. That is what Iris decided best describes her daughter's annoyingly cheerful voice: she tweets. "One Irish cream. One hazelnut. And this one's cinnamon."

"I would give anything for real coffee," Iris grumbles. "Or better yet, a Manhattan."

Mallory's face crumples like a used Kleenex.

"Really, Mom," Gwendolyn says without looking up from her papers, "it's only ten o'clock."

"There is no time in here," Iris says. Wait. She has two 4s in the same row? She throws the book onto the table with its mauve plastic water pitcher, blue plastic bedpan, and TV remote control.

"Well, I'll try the cinnamon," Mallory says in her tweety, can-do way.

"Give Mom the Irish cream," Gwendolyn says. "She can pretend it's Bailey's."

Iris takes the coffee, sips it, and grimaces.

"Has the doctor been in already?" Mallory asks.

"Yes," Iris says patiently. "He's dying."

Mallory looks stricken, as if this were the first time she'd heard the news. "He can hear you, you know," she stage whispers.

All Iris needs to completely ruin the morning is for Charlotte to show up, which of course she does as soon as Iris thinks this. Iris tries to remember the last time she saw Charlotte in something other than maternity clothes, and she can't. The girl just keeps having babies, one after the other. Iris supposes she shouldn't be judgmental about it. At least Charlotte has given her grandchildren. Gwendolyn got divorced before she bothered to have any children, and Mallory hasn't even bothered to get married.

Charlotte kisses her father on the forehead. "Hello, handsome," she says. She eyeballs the one unclaimed cup of coffee. "Decaf?" she asks.

Mallory looks offended. "I didn't know you were coming," she says. Is she actually going to cry over this? Iris wonders.

"I come every morning after I drop Cooper at nursery, and I stay until I have to pick up Sophie and Quinn." Charlotte takes out her knitting and gets to work. "I don't know why that's so hard to remember."

"We're not all as perfect as you, I guess," Mallory says.

Iris closes her eyes. She wishes that when she opened them, the girls would all be gone, back to their lives: Gwendolyn talking about obscure movies to college students and Mallory cleaning people's teeth and Charlotte baking a week's worth of bread and Iris herself, in her own living room with the matching Ethan Allen furniture and the coffee table they bought in Morocco, sipping a perfect Manhattan.

She opens her eyes and everything is just the same. Toby's machines pump and ding. Charlotte's knitting needles click ever so softly. Out in the hall, an intercom calls for a doctor. *Just die,* Iris tells her husband. Such a simple thing. People do it every day with no fanfare. Not Toby. He just keeps living.

Five months earlier, on the most ordinary July day, Toby walked into the kitchen, pale and sweaty. He usually got home at six; Iris could set her watch by his arrival. But he walked in at 5:15 and immediately poured himself a big shot of bourbon. Iris was stuffing herbed goat cheese under the skin of boneless chicken breasts.

"Something unbelievable has happened," Toby said. He took a swallow of bourbon. He shook his head. "Maybe you should have some of this," he said.

Trembling, Iris got another glass and poured herself a hefty shot.

"Remember, I saw the doctor about that backache I can't seem to get rid of?"

Iris nodded.

"I thought I wrenched it helping Mallory move that dresser," he said.

"And?" Iris asked impatiently. If she didn't get the potatoes in the oven, they wouldn't be done in time. Gwendolyn was bringing a new beau for dinner at 6:30. Another strange academic type, no doubt. But Iris still wanted to give them a nice meal.

"And it's pancreatic cancer," Toby said, as if it was a marvelous thing.

At a bridge night just a few months before, pancreatic cancer was the very thing they had all agreed was the one they didn't want to get. "That one's a death sentence," Oscar had said. And he should know. He'd had prostate and bladder cancer already. June and Margie had both had breast cancer. Steve had some kind of skin cancer, not melanoma but another kind that required constant surgery on his nose. "I think I would take lung cancer over pancreatic," Buzz had said. Hadn't everyone nodded in agreement? Anything was better than pancreatic cancer.

Iris didn't even realize that she had taken Toby's hand and was clutching it as if her life depended on it, as if his hand was her lifeline.

"Oh, Toby," she said. She supposed she should call Gwendolyn and cancel dinner. She should turn off the asparagus, which were boiling to nothing on the stove and sending a urine smell throughout the kitchen. But she couldn't get up and do anything. She could just sit there and hold her husband's hand.

"How's our Energizer Bunny?" a nurse says as she bustles in.

Iris wonders why nurses wear such ugly uniforms these days. Her best friend Junie was a nurse way back when, and she wore a starched white uniform, nipped at the waist, neatly buttoned, with a perky hat. These nurses wear powder blue or dusty rose, baggy things. Or worse, like this one, a mustard yellow one with teddy bears all over it. No hat.

Mallory follows the nurse through her routine checking of things: IVs and blood pressure and blood ox levels.

"Do you work in the health care field?" the nurse asks. She says it politely, but Iris can't help but think Mallory is bothering her.

"Yes, I do," Mallory says.

Gwendolyn snorts.

"I'm a dental hygienist," Mallory says, glaring with her teary eyes.

The nurse nods. "That's one I don't think I could handle," she says, making notes. "Working in someone's mouth like that."

Iris stifles a chuckle. Here is a woman who deals with all sorts of bodily fluids every day and can't imagine cleaning someone's teeth. It takes all kinds, she supposes.

"You can't imagine how poorly some people treat their teeth," Mallory is saying.

Charlotte says, "We make it a routine at our house. You have to start early." She doesn't even pause in her knitting. Iris watches the yarn fly from one needle to the other, back and forth.

"You have little ones?" the nurse says. She is measuring Toby's urine output, and frowning.

"Four," Charlotte says "And another one due in November."

The nurse tsks. Iris tries to determine if she is reacting to the ridiculous number of children Charlotte has or to Toby's urine.

"How's he doing?" Iris asks hopefully.

The nurse shakes her head. "Kidneys are sluggish," she says. She holds up the bag that hangs low on the side of the bed.

"So he's worse?" Iris asks.

The nurse considers this. "Oh, Mrs. Wilcox, you know it's just a matter of time. I'm so sorry."

"But how much more time?" Iris says.

"I can't say for sure," the nurse says, confused.

Mallory has started to whimper.

"Nerves get frayed, don't they?" the nurse says. She sympathetically rubs Mallory's back.

Charlotte rolls up her yarn and stands. "Call me if something changes," she says. And like clockwork, she leaves to pick up Sophie and Quinn, pausing to smooth her father's stubbly hair.

Even as a child, Charlotte was orderly. She arranged her clothes by color and alphabetized her books.

"His pressure's a bit low," the nurse says, frowning. "I'm going to page the doctor."

For the first time in months, Iris feels almost lighthearted. Of course, there have been false alarms these past months. They all rushed to the hospital in the middle of the night, with bed hair and sour breath, only to find that death had been averted while they careened down Route 95. But those times, Toby was awake, practically alert. It had been weeks since he'd opened his eyes or uttered even a word. This time, surely, would be different.

At first, they were brave warriors. "We can fight this," they said. "We can win." Even as the stone-faced doctors, one specialist at a time, told them they could not, Toby and Iris did not waver. At night, in the queen-size bed they had been wanting to upgrade to a king forever, they still made love and whispered together about the future. Except this new future involved experimental treatments and appointments with doctors at Johns Hopkins and Emory and someplace in Houston. Toby dutifully went to work every day, assessing other people's life indexes. Somehow, in their march forward, Iris didn't notice that Toby had grown thinner and faintly yellow. Until the day she did.

Late August, six weeks and dozens of doctor's appointments and treatments and procedures later, Iris grilled flank steak marinated in Good Seasons Italian dressing for dinner. She placed it on a platter, then turned to hand it to Toby to carve. He always carved. At first, she thought it was the fading afternoon light that made his skin seem that strange color. But as he moved toward her, she saw that his pants drooped from his hips and the whites of his eyes also had that pale, almost pretty, yellow cast. That very night he was hospitalized for the first time.

Hospital trips became routine, but he always came home eventually. With new pills, a scarier prognosis, thinner, weaker, but home. Boxes of Ensure lined the pantry. Still, Iris made dinners with all the food groups in them. She rented movies. They played bridge.

Then, right before Thanksgiving, when the air had turned chilly and stayed that way and the trees had gone completely bare, a doctor looked at the two of them and said, matter-of-factly but not unkindly, two weeks, a month at the most. They have not left the hospital since.

That night, alone in the hospital room with the lights low and the hallways quiet, Iris and Toby made peace with what was coming. They loved each other, had loved each other since they were both round-faced college sophomores at Northwestern, struggling through probability and statistics. They'd had a good life, fine daughters, dear friends. "Lucky," Toby whispered to her. "Lucky, lucky us."

Outside, it is winter, gray and cold. Iris knows this only because of the calendar that hangs on the wall and the way darkness arrives early and stays put. In this room, there is no air, no sun, no sense of time. Her daughters dress in fleece and mittens and hats that Charlotte has knit them. But to Iris, it is not winter. It is nothing.

Someone has placed a small Christmas tree at the nurses' station, hung shiny tinsel and red plastic garland on its skinny branches. Iris fights the memory of all the years of trips to the country to choose a Christmas tree. They always got a Douglas fir and argued over which was the most perfect one. She thinks of the empty corner of the parlor where those trees always stood, the star on top losing its glitter over time.

"Mom," Mallory says, touching Iris' arm.

"I was just thinking about Christmas. I guess we won't be getting a tree this year," Iris says.

"The doctor's here, Mom," Mallory says.

The doctor has an accent that Iris has to struggle to understand. Gwendolyn scolds her for this, as if she were doing it on purpose.

"He's glowing?" Iris asks him now.

The doctor frowns at her.

"Going," Gwendolyn says sharply.

"Ah," Iris says. "Today?"

Mallory cries at her father's bedside.

"I am not George," the doctor says.

Seeing her mother's confusion, Gwen says, "He's not God."

"Of course," Iris says.

When he leaves, Iris laughs. "I thought he said he wasn't George."

"You're being ethnocentric," Gwendolyn reprimands her.

"I am not," Iris insists, still laughing.

"Should we call Charlotte?" Mallory manages to say through her sobs.

"I hate to bother her," Iris says. "She has all those children."

"I think she uses them as an excuse to not be here," Mallory says.

This has not occurred to Iris. Charlotte and her knitting seem to be here all the time.

"And you use your classes, like they're more important than Daddy," Mallory says to Gwendolyn.

"It's the end of the semester!" Gwendolyn says. "I need to grade papers."

Mallory is full out crying now. "I found someone to cover for me," she says.

"It doesn't work that way," Gwendolyn mutters.

The nurse has marched back in, purposeful and serious now. Two doctors—at least, Iris thinks they're doctors—are right behind her. They both study the chart, pointing and whispering. When one of them catches Iris' eye, his face fills with pity.

From somewhere down the hall, Christmas carols are sung. It seems incongruous to Iris, carolers and Christmas trees and all these sick people.

The singing grows nearer.

Gwendolyn says, "What is that?"

"I think it's nice," Mallory says.

"The candy stripers," one of the doctors says apologetically.

"I think I'll go to the coffee cart," Iris says. She does not like the feeling rising in her chest. Everything is off kilter. She and Toby said their goodbyes, yet here she is, trapped in this cocoon of illness. She wants to walk out of this room, out of this hospital, into the winter afternoon.

"Want company?" Gwendolyn asks.

Iris shakes her head and walks out of the room, fast, almost knocking over a pigtailed caroler clutching her songbook.

The girl takes a breath and sounds a note on a pitch pipe. Carolers surround Iris.

"God bless ye merry gentlemen," they sing, "let nothing you dismay…"

Don't you know people are dying in here? Iris thinks, but she just pushes her way through them and down the hall, past the Christmas tree and the nurses. There is a bowl of candy canes on the desk, and

Ann Hood 73

cheap felt stockings with names in gold glitter hung there. Iris pauses. The calendar page is a big twenty-four. Christmas Eve and somehow Iris has forgotten all about the holiday until now.

She makes her way through the empty corridors to the coffee cart and buys a peppermint, a gingerbread, and an eggnog coffee. The smell of the too sweet flavorings fills her nose, inexplicably bringing a rush of memories to her: the children on sleds, Toby stringing twinkling blue lights in their hedges, the two of them beside the tree on Christmas Eve building doll houses and play kitchens. Grief overtakes her. Iris sits down, trying to catch her breath.

The intercom crackles. "Code Blue. Code Blue."

Nurses and doctors appear from nowhere, racing down the hall in a flurry of flying stethoscopes and pastel scrubs.

"No!" Iris hears herself yell. She jumps to her feet, the coffee falling from her lap and spilling onto the linoleum floor.

Iris is running too now, calling to her husband: "Toby! Wait! Toby!"

Everyone disappears around the corner.

"Toby!" Iris shouts.

When she finally reaches his room, she expects to find doctors and chaos. She expects to find him gone.

But the room is quiet. Mallory sits on her father's bed, humming "Silent Night." Gwendolyn sits correcting papers and Charlotte is back, knitting again. In the distance, the carolers are singing faintly. It is growing dark, but no one has turned on any lights. Snow has begun falling outside, lazy fat flakes. Toby's chest rises and falls, rises and falls.

Iris stands in the doorway, taking it all in. Husband. Daughters. Winter. Song. For this moment, Iris has everything. And she is grateful.

JOSHUA HOWES
Run

This is a story about pretending. Imagine my father, a boy, not the old man who bought this shuttered house I have just cleaned out, here at the tropical tip of Florida, but a boy of six, seven, eight, in a one-room school with snow-bent eaves, with another black eye, another chipped tooth, pretending he's fallen from a tractor again or was kicked by a horse. And imagine my father at fifteen, skinny, scared, his neck burnt red, running from farm and foster farm—explaining to kids who might have been friends, "My mother don't like me to have folks to the house" (in truth he's living in the shuttered dairy factory on the edge of town). And my father, at nineteen, pretending to be a college student, migrated to the smokestack city of fifty thousand on the river, where he's actually taking college classes, pretending to read books he's actually read, pretending to write papers he's actually written, and pretending not to work, pretending his parents also send money to the bank account he's never opened, hustling from class to the truck stop on US 61, where he'll spend 8:00 p.m. to 4:00 a.m. changing tires, tires as heavy as oil drums, twice the size of the scrawny roughneck quick-pumping the iron accordion of the rusted toothy jack. Pretending to the truckers, the shiftless alcoholic whites, the clannish blacks, the quiet Mexicans, that he also has never been to or even seen the college on the other side of the river. And imagine my father, at twenty-one, growing his curly hair and dreaming of San Francisco, raising his own tender marijuana plants in a basement, only for show because he's never smoked it, and lingering awake past dawn reading Joyce and Pound beside the space heater, wrapped in wool against the freezing Upper Midwest solitude, pretending to be the kind of intellectual who knows what the hell he's reading when he's reading Joyce.

My god, I imagine him, at twenty-two, walking away from his graduation, with the roar of alcoholic celebration fading to dullness beneath the hum of factories behind him, walking out onto the bridge above the dark-rolling river, the river that laps like an endless tongue at the banks of the land, standing on the bridge and holding up against all that darkening empty land, that darkening sky as huge and empty as the land, and his darkening past as huge and empty as both, the bright fantastical conception of his future, all his pretending rolled into a singular notion, a dream to which he will be ever faithful. And I imagine my father, the pool-playing kid, alone, with his college degree, breaking down and crying, above the indifferent coursing of the ancient Mississippi.

This is a story about pretending. I think of my father, imagine him at twenty-four, twenty-five, wooing my mother, reading her Provençal poetry but knowing how to fix the carburetor on her Ford, only one of these an act of pretending, and I think of my father at thirty-four, thirty-five, opening another patient's chest, cracking the sternum, harvesting thoracic arteries, suturing cannulae, instructing the perfusionist, and asking the CNA to flip the tape and restart Mozart (Piano Sonata No. 11 in A Major). My father has ugly hands, they are neither tapered nor uncallused, but what is vital, they are dead as ice—in forty years of pretending to be a surgeon, he will never make a mistake with them. He will pretend to save thousands of lives, pretend to train hundreds of younger doctors, pretend to write thousands of pages in the medical literature. He will take his children from Chicago to Europe, Africa, Asia; he will marvel with them that it is also his first time in these exotic places, his first trips over the vastness of the oceans by jet; he will whisper to his children, "This pyramid was built by Cheops in 2,500 BC" or "Michelangelo nearly went blind painting this ceiling by candlelight," and his children will never know he is pretending. He is not the sort of person who has heard of Cheops or Michelangelo, he is only making up the story of his life and theirs on the fly, skipping like a flat gray stone on the surface of his existence, terrified that should he ever slow, he will stop, turn over once, and sink.

But he never slows; he takes his grandchildren to these same places (his children could never afford to), he directs entire wings of hospitals, cuts ribbons to open the green flanks of parks, writes letters to the editor pretending to be the kind of citizen who cares what the government does for veterans with traumatic brain injuries. Just last year, I visited him here in Florida, the first since Mom died, and saw him still pretending, as always, to know how to play golf, cook Italian, sing a cappella to the patients at St. Luke's, and sail the Intracoastal. And I saw him musing at breakfast over the portrait of my mother, his wife, later his ex, at whose altar he worshipped for decades, even through all the long years after she told him she couldn't stand to live in the same house with him any longer. And I said, "What're you thinking?" He, "That we'd better get going or we'll miss our tee time."

So your heart remains, like the hearts of all fathers, unrecoverable, a shade-breeding light that shrouds its source. How I once tried to pry your briefest cracks, to peer into that source, the drunken time you muttered, "Poor Jimmy Klatchky, dead bastard I killed..." when? in surgery? on a winding road? or in the abandoned factory at night, a flicker of knife, an ugly sound, the scratching of heels on an iron floor? But I should stop imagining. Or that last brief furious fight, when Mom found a basket in the attic and burned it in a pile in the yard while you cuffed me back inside so I couldn't see. Or that other, older mother, yours, the woman in the picture with the funny glasses, her death the only time I saw you cry. I followed you to the alley dumpster, carrying a violin, a sled, a pair of pumps, an old frayed shawl, I confronted you and you laughed with a gleam of wild river in your eyes and I turned away, afraid. How in the end, I learned to love you like a hero in a film—with a love that depends on our never seeing the actor after the lights are dimmed, his makeup stripped away, haunting the habitudes of his driftless solitude, plotting the next day's work. How in these late, last years, I have tried to learn to be like you, in these minor scribblings, my own pale mimicries, to re-create what was never created.

So this is a story about pretending. Mine and his. My father, who, in a lifetime of neverending lies and pretense, I think spread enough good across this benighted world to turn the very act of lying into truth—effected, by the simple frightened fidelity of his conception of himself to himself, the transubstantiation of vulgarity to grace, the meretricious to the dear, the winter dark to the summer light—until that dreary November afternoon his fear caught up with him, working in the barn on his refurbished ancestral Wisconsin land—he saw in the darkening window, lit by dying light, the likeness of a black-eyed, dirty-cheeked six-year-old running scared.

Joshua Howes

CAMPBELL McGRATH
An Irish Word

Canny has always been an Irish word
to my ear, so too its cousin *crafty,*
suggesting not only an appreciation of close-work,
fine-making, handwrought artistry,

but a highly evolved reliance on one's wits to survive,
stealth in the shadow of repressive institutions,
"silence, exile, and cunning," in Joyce's admonition,
ferret-sly, fox-quick, silvery, and elusive.

Craft, akin to *croft*—
a shepherd's crooked hawthorn staff,
wind-polished wolds and peat-spent moorlands
high in the Blue Stack Mountains.

Akin to *draught*—a pint of creamy stout
or a good stout draught horse
or a draughty old house
like the one in which my grandfather was born

near Drimnaherk, slate-roofed, hard-angled,
ringed by thistles in a soil-starved coomb.
His four brothers left home
bound for Australia, South Africa, Liverpool, and Los Angeles

losing track of each other at once and forever
as if to loose the hawsers and set sail
were to sever every filial tether.
His name was Francis Daniel Campbell

but my grandmother Anna was a Monaghan
and her people had been
Maguires, Morans, Mohans, Meehans,
and other alliterative, slant-rhymed clans

all the way back to the nameless
bog dwellers and kine folk.
When her father died suddenly in New York,
he left three baby daughters and a widowed seamstress

with no recourse but retreat
to the old Rose Cottage overlooking Donegal Bay
in a parish of trellised thorns and ricked hay,
taking in mending and needlework to eat.

Market days they rode the train into Derry
to sell embroidered linens and hand-tatted lace,
kerchiefs monogrammed *z* to *a*.
She was nearing thirty

when she married and recrossed the Atlantic
and from her my own mother
had a recipe for soda bread, piles of drop-stitch
tablecloths, and a small stoneware pitcher

hand-painted in folksy script—
Be Canny Wi' the Cream.
Nothing could move my brother and I to screams
of laughter like that tiny pitcher,

so serious of purpose, so quaintly archaic,
as we slurped down bowls of Frosted Flakes
before school in the breakfast nook.
The scrupulous economy of the world it bespoke,

the frugality toward which it gestured,
were as inscrutable to us then
as the great sea cliffs at Slieve League when
we drove to the top at Amharc Mór

on a road so thickly fleeced with mist
we might have been lost if not for the sheep
materializing like guardian imps,
imperturbable creatures, black-faced ephreets,

the ocean one vast, invisible gong
struck by padded mallets or mailed fists.
Amharc Mór means "the grand view" in Irish
but all we saw was fog.

CAMPBELL McGRATH
The Fly

As for the fly I chased around the bathroom with a towel that night,
   swatting, slapping, thrashing, pounding,
kicking with one foot the toothbrush cup onto its side, dislodging the
   tea curtain with a misplaced elbow,
unable for all my efforts to terminate his gallant loops and arabesques,
   his beeline dives and fighter-pilot vectorings,
his stalls and silences, his crafty retreats, his increasingly erratic bursts
   toward any open corner or avenue of escape,
behind the toilet, above the shower rod, inside the light wells, disappearing like a magician only to reappear again and again—
as for the fly, our struggle went on a long time. Too long. It was already
   after midnight when it began, the house calm,
everything dark beyond our gladiatorial arena, crazy to bother, ridiculous to carry on, but I was determined to finish it.

And when he stopped at last, gone for good, the body unseen but certainly dead, pulverized at a blow, squashed and unrecoverable
when that silence was assured I felt certain of a conquest too small to
   call a triumph but a victory nonetheless.

And when, the next day, lifting a fresh towel from the bar, he fell to the
   floor, not dead but irreparably damaged,
lurching, toppling, lopsided, wing-still, no longer jittering with defiance, no longer challenging fate with desperate brio,
when I discovered him then everything had changed, and we were no
   longer fated to deadly opposition,
no longer entranced by the simplicity of our struggle, and I no longer
   understood the antagonism of the night before,
felt entirely alien from it, felt now that it was a perturbing frenzy, a kind
   of madness that had possessed me.

Which did not mean that he did not have to die, only that it was not,
    or not anymore, an act of murder but a cost of war,
or so I told myself, adorned in the common skin of my kind, naked
    before the mirror in the exalted light of morning.

RACHEL KADISH
The Governess and the Tree

> "Is anything—not even happiness but just not torment—possible? No, nothing!" she answered herself now without the least hesitation. "...All efforts have been made; the screw is stripped."
> —Anna in Leo Tolstoy's *Anna Karenina*

> "She's writing a book for children and doesn't tell anybody about it, but she read it to me, and I gave the manuscript to Vorkuev...He's a good judge, and he says it's a remarkable thing."
> —Stepán Arkádyevich Oblonsky, regarding his sister, Anna

> "My writing is like those little carved baskets made in prisons..."
> —Anna

Once, in the woods, a tree.

Once in the woods there was a tree with the power to tell the future. The children of the household yearned for its verdicts on their lives, but their governess was wiser.

Give me your tokens, the governess said to the children, and I will take them to the tree and ask your fortune. Then if the tree should become angry, it will be not you but I standing before it.

Although the children had never seen their governess smile in all the years she'd taught them their lessons, still they loved her stern face with a great and terrible love, the love of children and untamed things. So the children gave her their tokens: a riding crop, a scrap of fine white lace, and a ribbon.

The governess, unsmiling as ever, gathered the children's tokens and put them in a pouch. Then she set off for the woods, promising to return soon with their fortunes.

But she had not told the children all. For the governess knew this tree, and in her own girlhood had stood before it with her heart full of hope. She knew that although the tree could tell fortunes, it was also a servant of the hag Baba Yaga, who often lay in wait inside it, and the governess had been seeking the tree these many years, for this tree moved from place to place along with Baba Yaga and her hut that stood on chicken legs.

The governess walked through the woods. The sun was setting, the time was neither day nor night, when she found the beautiful silvery tree and stood before it.

"I have come, gentle tree, to learn the fortunes of the children in my charge," she said.

Hidden inside the tree, old Baba Yaga awoke from her nap and looked through a knothole at the governess. Now Baba Yaga's fingers were of yellow bone with talons like a bird's, and her eyes were yellow and her neck was as thin as a snake. She had teeth of metal for crushing the bones of those who trusted her.

There was something about the well-dressed governess with her erect posture that seemed familiar to Baba Yaga—the curls of dark hair at the temples, the small white hands. But Baba Yaga put on her sweetest voice and spoke through the tree to the governess, and the tree swayed its silvery boughs in welcome.

"Give me a token," Baba Yaga said, in the dulcet well-bred voice that was agony for her to speak.

The governess held out the riding crop that had been given her by the eldest child. "Here, gentlest tree," she said, "is a token from the eldest, a boy of eleven. He wishes to know his future."

But when the bone hand of Baba Yaga reached through a knot in the tree, the governess, knowing who it was that reached toward her, did not step forward. "I am nearly blind," the governess lied. "In this poor light I cannot see you. You must come to me to take the token, tree spirit."

Baba Yaga hesitated. Something was familiar about this governess, but she needed another moment to recollect it. "Show me the other tokens," she sang.

The governess produced them from her pouch. She held up the lace. "This is from a girl of nine who wishes to know what the world holds for her."

Baba Yaga sensed all was not as it seemed, but she was greedy, and

84 *Ploughshares*

the white lace gleamed in the twilight like a tissue of sewn pearls.

"Have you any other tokens?" she said, her throat aching with the effort of such modulated speech.

"Only this velvet ribbon," said the governess, producing the ribbon and dangling it before the tree. "It belongs to a girl of seven. But her future will be told by me and not you."

Angered at this, Baba Yaga at last stepped from the tree.

And indeed, she now believed the governess to be blind, for all people recoiled when they first saw Baba Yaga's form, but the governess did not flinch as Baba Yaga stepped toward her in the half-light. Again the hag thought there was something familiar about this governess, yet she knew not what.

The governess, though, knew Baba Yaga, and she was ready. For in her girlhood many years ago the governess, too, had learned of a fortune-telling tree that gave fortunes both beautiful and frightening, and she had ventured with her friends to the woods to seek its wisdom. And the tree had seemed to her to be kind, and it had spoken in such silvery tones that none could fail to heed it.

Yet although the friends that were with her that long-ago evening had been envious of the fortune the tree had whispered to her, which unlike theirs contained no hint of sorrow to furrow her brow, she herself had been displeased, for the fortune she had been given told of order and quiet and a love that was neither great nor terrible. The girl could not sleep that night for the feeling this fortune gave her, as though all the loneliness in the world were pressing on her heart from the inside, and she felt her heart grow cold and heavy as it beat on pointlessly in her chest, and it seemed to her that her life had ended when it had hardly begun. And so she rose the next day and returned to the tree despite the pleas of her friends, for she was a bold child and much loved in her home—and because nothing had ever been denied her, she had never felt the sting of reprimand nor the need for shame.

Reaching the tree for the second time in two days, she'd curtseyed and said to it, I seek another fortune, if you please.

And with a crack of thunder Baba Yaga sprang from it, and the girl fell to the earth certain that she would die on that spot of fright.

Baba Yaga had just that hour eaten a full meal of six sheep and a hare, so instead of seizing the girl to eat her she laughed a laugh that shredded the air, and raised a bone finger. "If you wish another fortune," she crowed, "then you may share mine."

In that instant the girl was cursed, and though she ran from that place back to her home, from that day her life was altered, and at the mere sight of her, former companions knew she was no longer as they were. For when she opened her mouth to speak or smile they saw that her teeth were made of metal, this being the curse Baba Yaga had set upon her—that the girl's beautiful face be forever marred by metal teeth such as those that gnashed in Baba Yaga's own mouth. There were other changes as well that had happened in the girl, though these could not be seen. All felt there was something unnatural now in her, and even her family faltered when defending her against the talk of society. A great shame seized the girl so that she wished to hide, but she defied it and went proudly abroad in the streets of her town as had been her custom, for in her heart this girl knew she'd done nothing but follow the path life had laid for her. Yet all doors were now closed against her, and when she had grown enough to set out on her own, she moved to a new village where none knew her, and she took work as a governess. Because she did not smile, none saw her teeth, and because the children both loved and obeyed her, the presence of her forbidding countenance soon became a mark of distinction among the best families.

Now she stood once again opposite the hag Baba Yaga, no longer a girl but a grown woman, and the hag did not recognize her.

"The children's fortunes?" said the governess in a quiet voice.

"Very well," Baba Yaga said, and she spoke in her own harsh voice. But something about the governess made her uneasy, for she sensed there was some dangerous kinship between them.

"The first will marry and raise heirs and die a rich thick-headed old man mocked in private by those family who praise him to his face," said Baba Yaga. "The second will perish in childbed. The third, whose fortune I will tell despite your foolish defiance, will refuse advice, marry poorly, and die of the consequences of this great and terrible love."

The governess lifted her head. "I do not accept these fortunes."

And then Baba Yaga remembered. For only one had ever refused her fortune. Yet it was too late, for the governess had tricked her into leaving the tree.

The governess smiled for the first time, then, and Baba Yaga saw her metal teeth, and a feeling Baba Yaga had never had shuddered through her, and the feeling was fear. Quickly Baba Yaga summoned her mortar and pestle, which flew to her from where they had been hidden. Stepping into the mortar, she shot high into the sky, steering with her pestle until she'd reached the lowest clouds, from where she planned to plunge down to destroy her opponent. But the governess stepped onto a fallen log and raised the riding crop, and at the governess' bidding the crop beat the log viciously. The log flew high, carrying the governess into the dusk far above Baba Yaga, so that Baba Yaga could not see her amid the clouds. Then Baba Yaga dove under the cover of the treetops and called up her broom from its hiding place. Trailing it behind the mortar, she flew high once more, and with the broom she swept the stars from the sky until all that was left was a terrible blackness—for Baba Yaga's yellow eyes could see in the dark and she knew the governess could not, and she planned to attack the governess when she was blinded and finish her right then.

But the governess, flying on her log, took the scrap of lace, and as she ripped open the stitches each turned into a ball of pearly light, and these floated far and wide through the sky so the dusk was lit with their shine and Baba Yaga could not hide.

Never had the forest seen such a battle as then occurred. For the governess had cast off her shawl and now her metal teeth flashed and her own hands looked like bones in the darkness, and the two hags soared and cursed as they carried their battle from the sky to the land, and the forest floor shook with the boulders they threw at one another, and the fish jumped in the lake at the earth's shudderings. And a madness overtook the governess, and she taunted Baba Yaga with the suspicions that had been flung at her by society when she herself had been cursed: "In truth, I have eaten the children with these teeth you gave me," she screamed at the frightened Baba Yaga, "and I bring you these their tokens only to goad you, for it is you I will eat next."

A terror such as Baba Yaga had never felt seized her, for she was with her equal.

From the edge of the forest, a goods train whistled as it rolled heavily toward the town. "You may have your first fortune back," croaked Baba Yaga slowly, making a show of defiance. "The one I gave you when you were a child."

But the governess refused. "You will give me another, to my liking."

Then Baba Yaga was desperate, for she knew of no other fortune to give, other than the two she had already given the governess, and so she flew at the governess to kill her, but when she sank her claws into the governess' smooth cheek, the governess seized Baba Yaga's neck and began to choke the life from her.

Yet the moment her hands closed on the thin snakelike neck, the governess herself began to struggle grievously to draw breath, and she remembered that she and the hag now shared the same fortune, and one could not die without the other perishing as well.

She released Baba Yaga, and Baba Yaga fled for the shelter of the fortune-telling tree. But finding in her pouch the last token, the governess threw the velvet ribbon into the silvery branches.

In all the years that the tree had been Baba Yaga's servant, Baba Yaga had never given the tree so much as a string to wear. Now when Baba Yaga flew to its trunk, it did not admit her, but for the first time closed itself to her no matter how the hag gashed its trunk with her teeth.

The two women stood in the woods. The woods breathed about them, the dusk thickened and the land sighed as it cooled, and still the two stood. Then Baba Yaga turned her back. She crept to the lake, where she planned to turn into a crow and make her escape. But before she did, she glimpsed her reflection in the lake's still waters. There she saw the beauty that had been hers before she'd been cursed to be a woman shunned by the world, and there she saw the beauty that was still hers.

With a quiet moan of pain she turned into a crow and flapped into the dark.

The governess stanched and cleaned the blood from her face, and returned home. Upon her return the children were stricken by the claw marks on her cheek, but she shushed them and said only that a breeze had risen while she was having her audience with the tree and its waving branches had scratched her. The children stared at the marks and were uncertain whether to believe, but greed for their fortunes swayed the two elder and they pressed their suit, pulling the youngest with them despite the puzzlement on the child's face. Together they crowded the governess, each beseeching in his or her own way: what is my fortune, dearest Nana. For this is what they had called her always, not knowing her true name.

The governess had ever loved these children, though their small concerns wearied her at times. And she saw that they wondered at the change that had come over her, though they had no words for it.

To the eldest she said, "I have spoken to the tree and have earned the power to give you this fortune: You will have the fate of Baba Yaga: to have many servants who must obey you. Only mind they do not simply obey but also love you, for the time will come when you will need their love most of all."

To the second, she said, "You will have the fate of Baba Yaga: to live without children. Tell any who woo you that you cannot bear a child, for there are ways to make this come to pass. So you will live and not die, and if a man marry you, he chooses you alone."

Then the children's mother, innocent and soft as a kitten, came into the room. Her hands worked reflexively at the sight of the governess, for she had never trusted the woman and had put her children in the governess' care only on the strong advice of those in the best circle of society, who had praised the governess ever since she appeared in their midst and declared her severe intelligence and strange silent dignity fashionable. The children's mother had employed the governess against her own better instincts, for she had ever found her monstrous, and she feared her.

So the mother watched closely now from across the nursery. Still, the governess turned her back on the mother and bent over the smallest girl (it was she whose ribbon had won the heart of the tree). And to this child the governess said, "You will be as I, and you will learn to fight for your fate, and you will reject two fortunes and make your own."

In the days thereafter, the riding crop became a large leather cloak, and the governess was always protected from even the bitterest cold in this outlandish covering, and all of society could recognize her striking figure from a distance. The pearly lace was never seen again, yet from that day onward the governess' teeth were no longer metal but pearls. They glimmered the whitest white, and none who looked upon them could help admiring their elegance, though many thought it frightening, and in the privacy of sleep some found their dreams haunted more fearsomely by that glimmering smile than by all the metal teeth of the hag Baba Yaga.

But the ribbon she gave to the girl.

JENNIFER MILITELLO
Antidote with Placebo

Pit yourself against gutted ships, against
the lips of those you love the least, against
the hollows where quails spend their lives.

Do not sleep. Do not take shape.
Ambush the soft armies of seas and the singular
face of an adjacent cliff. Scream the way

everything screams. Find a small longitude
to stitch along the coast. Find an iodine
to dye your dreams. Find a decade. Deny

your face. Deny the very steps you take,
three times before the cock crows.
Never pace. Never betray your need.

Never drink the nocturne's blood.
Become a lion who obeys the whip, become
a tiger in a cage. Become the rage that never fits,

the metal, the release. Challenge yourself against
the streets. Cradle your head in your hands.
Be chaste. Drop a kerchief from a windowed

train. See yourself as a curb blurred by water,
stagnant, layered in grease. Grow untender.
Grow corrupt. Strangle your reason to within

an inch of its life. Focus like a machine.
Then find the city, the stink of steam.
The soft demeaning face of light

the traffic will give off. Grab the distance
from your heart and rust with it in
your hand. Understand the starve

and feast. Understand the stop and start.
The slaughter. The plea for release.
Drop the suit of your self with its solitary pelt

and debris of autumn leaves, with its chrome
to row through and feel alive, with its miles
as herons on a lake. Soon you will wake,

so doctor your corpse. Let the scissors
scathe you to lyres. Operate while it's still day.
Then drop the body onto its clockwork of joints,

onto its lace of nerves, onto the curves
of its spine and its place. Check for breath
at the entrance of its arch. Check for breath

at the gangway of its waist. Let it drop
once you have worshipped the nurture,
the circle of thorns it remains.

JOSEPH MILLAR
Late December

It's the day after Christmas
a flat gray morning where the rain
has fallen on the crooked streets
and no one has stolen our newspaper,
its headline denouncing the young Nigerian,
someone's devout beloved son
who tried to blow up a plane,
my own son half asleep on the couch
in his Levis and unraveled socks,
his brother still out looking for work
and the sound of coughing on the back stairs
like the ghost of Edna St. Vincent Millay.
Now the horses of North Carolina
bend down to drink
from their starry pond
having listened all night to the spacecraft
hovering like metal angels
over the fields and tobacco barns,
their plutonium shutters and platinum fins,
their calamitous holy light.

MARGE PIERCY
The night has a long hairy pelt

The night is tall and strewn with rocks
cutting my feet as I climb, panting
under the blankets, the quilt.
Will it ever be light again?

I hear sounds outside, footsteps
that I hope are a deer's cloven
hooves. Coywolves in the marsh
shriek like banshees over a kill.

What, I think, is a banshee, exactly?
As a child I saw skulls at the tip
of the open door, monsters rustled
under the bed with green teeth.

This bedroom is crawling with unpaid
bills white as maggots. Words
spoken harshly make my skin itch.
Morning's sun is miles away.

The night is endless, stretching
like train tracks to the flat horizon.
Weeds sprout between every minute.
Darkness nourishes them to trees.

The first gray mist almost thins
the air. After a while the shape
of a dogwood outside the window
firms itself. The waking birds cry.

The monsters have left the bed.
The dresser is just furniture. Color
seeps back into the world. See:
morning surrounds us at last.

MARGE PIERCY
The romantic getaway

We live alone together
except for five cats, yet
sometimes the only way
to be truly alone
is to run away together.

Away from the computer,
e-mail, Facebook, the cell
phone, the land line,
meetings, the endless list
of things to be done—

that no matter how many
I cross off, keeps growing
so that my love says
his tombstone will read
he had more stuff to do.

The list is an anaconda.
The list is a self
perpetuating monster
that gives birth constantly
like a queen ant

sending us workers
scurrying. We must
sneak away from home
and pay for an empty
room to be truly alone.

MARGE PIERCY
Baggage

It surprises me that immigrants brought
rootstock of roses in their luggage.
Scots roses, spinosissima, Eglanteria,
the briar rose that spread out into
New England: bits of thorny fragrance
that smelled like home. Mostly
they were at least as tough
as the people who carted them here.

I can understand seeds of grain,
of vegetables, rootstock of fruit
and nut trees, but roses? I see
some goodwife carefully cutting,
packing in linens what she hoped
would bloom beside her newly
built door. In spring, carefully
tucked into the strange soil.

What we cherish makes sense
only to us. I keep for decades
a china dog and cat I played with
in a battered dollhouse, making
stories that were my first
inventions. They remind me
where I started and with what,
who I was when I first was me.

WALLY LAMB
Girl Skipping Rope

I was born in the Tuscan city of Siena, and among my earliest and fondest memories is having sat long ago on my father's lap at a table outside the Piazza del Campo, with the Fountain of Gaia gurgling nearby, watching, wide-eyed, as Papa's pencil turned blank paper into cartoon animals on my behalf. His ability to do so had seemed magical to the little boy I was. But sadly, my parents fell on hard times after my father's tailor shop was burned to the ground by the vengeful husband of his mistress.

"Manhattan has thousands of businessmen and they all need suits," my Uncle Nunzio assured his destitute brother in a letter he wrote to him after the fire. "Come." Nunzio had enclosed money too: enough American dollars for three passages to New York. And so Papa, Mama, and I left Siena, boarded a ship at the port in Livorno, and voyaged across the wide, wide water. Twelve days later, we passed La Statua della Libertà and arrived on American soil. This was February 1921. I was eight years old. Years later, after my own manly desires had awakened, Papa confided to me that he had not wished to be unfaithful to my mother, but that his *innamorata*, Valentina, had a body by Botticelli and hair so flaming red that she might have stepped out of a painting by Titian. Tailoring was Papa's trade, but art was his *passione*.

From his youth to the time of our departure for America, my father had visited museums throughout Tuscany to gaze at the great works of Florentine and Sienese painters of the past—those renderings of Jesus and the saints, of the nobility of Roma and Venezia, the peasantry at work and play beneath the Tuscan sun. He'd stood before "David," the masterpiece Michelangelo had carved from a block of pure white Carrara marble at the tender age of twenty-six. "Gualtiero, I looked up and wept to think that that block of stone had spoken to the maestro," he told me once. "That the rock had said, 'Carve and you shall find the man within!'" Although Papa had had no formal training as an artist himself, he had a natural talent and an undeniable urge to draw and was seldom without his pencil and portfolio of onionskin paper. "A gift from God," my mother once called her husband's artistic talent, though she would later describe it as "my Giuseppe's curse."

In New York, we lived above Uncle Nunzio's grocery market in a four-story tenement on Spring Street. Nunzio knew someone who knew someone, and soon my father was altering men's suits at Macy's Department Store on Herald Square. While Papa was measuring inseams, sewing shoulder pads into suit coats, and letting out the trousers of well-fed businessmen, I was mastering proper English in the classrooms of the Catholic Sisters of the Poor Clares and learning broken English at Uncle Nunzio's grocery market, where I was employed after school and every Saturday. In warm weather, my job was to sell roasted peanuts from the barrel outside on the sidewalk. During the winter months, I was brought inside to wait on the kerchiefed *nonnas* who came by each day to shop for their families' dinners and haggle over the prices of fruit and vegetables. (Often these cagey women, Siciliani for the most part, would first bruise the fruit they had selected and then demand a reduced price because the fruit was bruised.)

At school, Sister Agatha took a shine to me and, because she thought I would make a good priest, urged me to pursue the sacrament of Holy Orders. But I was my father's son on two counts: first, when I was in the eighth grade, I surrendered my virginity to an experienced "older woman" of sixteen who was fond of roasted peanuts; and second, I loved to draw. Seated on a stool next to my peanut barrel, I would sketch the Packards and roadsters parked along Spring Street, the passersby rich and poor, the fluttering garments hanging from clotheslines across the street, the birds who flew in the sky, and the pigeons who waddled along the sidewalk, pecking away at morsels of food. I filled sketchbook after sketchbook, eager to show Papa my latest drawings when he returned home from his day of tailoring. My father smiled very little back then, but he beamed whenever he looked at my pictures.

When I was fifteen, one of my drawings won a prize: art lessons. And so each Saturday morning, freed from my job at Uncle Nunzio's, I would ride my bicycle up Fifth Avenue to the Metropolitan Museum of

Art, where I would receive instruction from a German painter named Victorious von Schlippe. Like Uncle Nunzio, Mr. von Schlippe knew people who knew people, and the following year, at the age of sixteen, I was offered a full scholarship to the prestigious school of the Art Institute of Chicago. With tears falling from her eyes, Mama begged me to stay in New York—to marry a nice Italian girl and give her grandchildren. Papa, on the other hand, urged me to go and learn whatever Chicago could teach me. The morning he saw me off at Grand Central Station, there were tears in his eyes too, especially after I unfolded the sheet of onionskin paper I'd slipped into my pocket when I packed that morning. "Look what I'm bringing, Papa," I said. He stood there, holding in his hands one of the cartoon drawings he had made for me years before. Then he handed it back to me, blew his nose, and told me I'd better board the train before it left without me. And so, without daring to look back at him, I did.

I loved the Windy City! Its crisp autumn weather, its warm and friendly people. I loved my classes too and was a sponge, absorbing whatever my instructors could teach me. On Sunday afternoons, it became my habit to write long letters to my parents about my exciting new life. But as autumn turned into winter, Mama's letters back to me began to describe a strange obsession that had overtaken my father. Papa claimed that Catherine of Siena, Italy's patron saint, had appeared to him in a dream, commanding him, for the edification of Italian Catholics the world over, to illustrate the story of her life: her service to the sick during the black death; her successful campaign to persuade Pope Gregory to return the papacy from Avignon to Rome; her receiving of the stigmata on her hands and feet. It was a terrible thing to witness, Mama wrote: a husband's strange decline into madness. "This week, he searches all over the city for a hair shirt, so that he might suffer as Saint Catherine suffered when she wore hers. And when he's not off on these wild goose chases, he wanders about the *appartamento,* mumbling nonsense to his precious saint. Ha! I have yet to hear her answer him!"

That Christmas, unable to afford the trip back home, I stayed in Chicago and sent my parents a gift box of candied fruit, nuts, and nougats. Presents arrived for me as well. Mama had sent me three pairs of thick socks and a week's supply of itchy woolen underwear. Papa's gift arrived in a long cardboard tube, and when I opened the end and uncurled the paper within, there was his charcoal rendering of the mystical marriage of Saint Catherine to Jesus Christ. In the foreground, along with the wedding couple, stood Mary Magdalene, Saints Dominic and John the Divine, and Mary, the Holy Queen of Heaven—who was now, apparently, Catherine's mother-in-law. Among the lesser wedding guests in the background, I spotted Papa and myself. The lines of my father's drawing, as bold and driven as the brushstrokes of the great van Gogh, illustrated a marriage of a different kind: the union between creation and madness. I pinned Papa's present to the wall above my bed, next to the fanciful drawing he had made for me when I was a little boy, and, looking from one to the other, lamented. If fate had been kinder to my father, I thought, he might have left New York, traveled west to California, and found work with the great Walt Disney instead of in a windowless back room at Macy's gentlemen's department. But as the people of the Old Country say, *Il destino dà le carte, ma chi le deve giocare siamo noi*. Destiny deals the cards, but it is we who must play them.

In January, Mama wrote that Papa no longer worked at Macy's, but it was unclear to her if he had resigned his position or been let go. "Hard to believe that tailoring had been his trade, Gualtiero, now that he skulks about, day after day, in the ragged shirt and frayed trousers he calls his 'working clothes.' They are his sleeping clothes too. He has not taken a bath or shaved in weeks, and it must be a month since that wild head of hair of his has felt a comb pass through it. Does he suffer, you ask. Oh yes, and *I* suffer too, Gualtiero, and I don't need a hair shirt to feel it!" She was forced now to go downstairs and work at Nunzio's store to make ends meet, Mama wrote. "All day long, I run the cash register and stock the shelves, ignoring as best I can my *gonfiore* and *emorroidi*, and slapping away the wandering hands of Nunzio's butcher, that goddamned Onofrio Buonocore. The other day, when he pinched me on the *culo*, I picked up a can of chi-chi beans and warned him. 'Stick to your salami slicing and sausage stuffing,' I said. 'Or else I'll clunk you on the *cocuzza* and make you sorry you didn't!' And I will too, Gualtiero. That son of a bitch had better not put me to the test or he'll end up with a bump on his noggin the size of a goose egg!"

Each week as I read my mother's letters, I sighed, wet-eyed—worried about Papa's craziness and Mama's bunions and hemorrhoids, her having to fend off Onofrio Buonocore's lecherous advances. But what could I do out here in Chicago? I telephoned Uncle Nunzio long-distance to ask if he thought I should return to New York. "No, no. Stay where you are and learn," he told me. "Your mother can take care of herself. And it is better you remember your father as he was than as he is now. Pray for him, light a candle now and then, and let me handle things here." And so, each morning on my knees, each afternoon as I walked along the lakeshore, and each night before I climbed into bed, I asked God to please grant my father a restful mind and my mother relief from bodily ailments and groping hands. For myself, I prayed for artistic inspiration.

At the art institute, I first copied the styles of the renowned artists of antiquity and the celebrated impressionists, expressionists, and pointillists of the previous century. But little by little, I began developing a style of my own, which one of my teachers, Frido Urbinati, described as "primitive yet painterly" and "boldly modern with a freshness of vision." I don't mean to boast, but I was generally recognized to be one of the three most promising students at the school, the others being my good friends, Bronx-born Antonio Orsini, who loved the New York Yankees more than life itself, and Wanda Kaszuba, an eccentric but affable Texan who wore cowgirl boots, smoked cigars, and swore like a man.

It was during my final year of study at the institute that, like Papa, I, too, became obsessed with a subject of my own: a nameless little Negro girl I spotted in Grant Park one afternoon while Antonio, Wanda, and I were eating our lunch. She was a lone figure in a shapeless gray dress, jumping rope and singing happily to herself. Her wiry hair was in plaits. Her face was turned up toward the sun in joyful innocence. My friends and I had been arguing about whether Roosevelt, the president-elect, would prove to be a savior or a scoundrel. As the others' voices faded away, I pulled a pencil from my pocket and sketched the rope-jumping girl on the oily paper in which my provolone and *sopressata* sandwich had been wrapped. Back at the studio, I drew her time and again, and then began painting her in gouache and oils, in primary colors and pastels and monochromatic shades of gray. It was as if this guileless child had bewitched me! I gave her a name, Fanny, and came to think of her as my muse.

For my final project, I submitted a series of sixteen works, collectively titled "Girl Skipping Rope." On graduation day, I held my breath as one of the institute's capped and gowned dignitaries announced, "And this year's top prize is awarded to…Gualtiero Agnello!" Sadly, Papa by then was too crazy to make the trip to Illinois, and Mama too timid to travel so far by train. So mine was a solitary triumph—but a triumph nonetheless.

I remained in Chicago for the next few years, eking out a living on Michigan Avenue from the small sums that wealthy passersby immune from the stock market crash paid me for the charcoal portraits I drew of them and their loved ones, and by shedding my clothes and posing as a figure model in the classrooms of the institute. (Luckily, nature had gifted me with a robust physique, which I further enhanced by sparring at a boxing club on East Lake Street, where I also rented a room.) During this time, I became friendly with many of the other young artists of the city, and with them enjoyed the bohemian life: the sharing of communal suppers made from our pooled ingredients, the drinking of cheap wine to excess as we engaged in heated arguments about what constituted great art, and nights of debauchery with a succession of willing women. In the midst of all this, quite unexpectedly, I fell in love.

Anja was a blond, blue-eyed Polish Jew who had crossed the Atlantic with her family in hopes that even a Depression-strapped America might afford them better economic opportunities than their homeland could. By day, Anja twisted her hair into a chignon and sold silk stockings and foundation garments behind a counter at Marshall Field's. At night, she let her hair down, disrobed, and, like me, earned extra money as an artist's model. Anja was demure and shy while posing, and at the cafés and bars where I would take her afterward. Yet when she climbed into my bed, a wild abandon would overtake her. We were married in City Hall shortly after the clinic doctor told us that the rabbit had died and Anja was pregnant.

During the Christmas season of 1932, I received a telegram from my mother, informing me that my father was on his deathbed and that I should hurry back to New York at once. I traveled east with my pregnant bride, intending that Anja and I would return to Chicago as soon as my father had been laid to rest. But Mama's prediction about Papa's impending demise was premature. He lingered for weeks and then months. By the time he succumbed in earnest, my landlady in Chicago had thrown out Anja's and my belongings and rented out our room. Anja was now in the eighth month of her pregnancy. One of Uncle Nunzio's customers, Dr. Alberto Quintiliani, had her walk up and down Spring Street so that he might assess her condition. Then he told us she must not travel.

Pride forbade me from borrowing more money from Uncle Nunzio as I had been doing, and so I registered with the State of New York as a Works Progress Administration artist. My affiliation with the WPA brought me good luck because, a short time later, I was assigned to assist the great Mexican painter Diego Rivera in the execution of his grand Rockefeller Center mural, "Man at the Crossroads." It was also at this time that I made the acquaintance of Rivera's wife, Frida Kahlo, who was his equal in artistic genius and artistic temperament. Once, during an evening of tequila drinking, I had to stand between the two to prevent their argument from turning into fisticuffs. (Diego told me that, although he was double the weight of his wife, he often got the worst end of these fights because, as a girl in Mexico, Frida had learned how to box.) Yet if Rivera and Kahlo were sometimes volatile with each other, mostly about his dalliances or hers, they also were deeply and passionately in love. To honor his wife, Diego painted Frida into his mural. But when he also painted the Bolshevik leader Vladimir Lenin into the work, he ignited a furor. His commission was promptly cancelled. "Bah! Water off the duck's back," Rivera scoffed as he packed for Chicago, where he had been commissioned to paint a mural for the Century of Progress Exposition. Diego and Frida invited me to go with them and I longed to return to my adopted city, but fatherhood came first. Anja had just given birth—not to a single chubby-cheeked infant, but to our three scrawny, squalling sons.

Worried that they might not survive, we hastily christened our babies Diego, Stanislaw, and Giuseppe—Diego in honor of the great

Rivera, the latter two in honor of Anja's and my own late fathers. Initially, my mother had not been happy about having acquired a daughter-in-law who was neither Italian nor Roman Catholic, but she and Anja, who at first barely tolerated each other, grew quite close after the babies were born and had been baptized. Mama got what she'd wished for after all: a son who had come back to her and given her grandchildren. She also acquired something she had *not* wished for: a second husband. Nunzio's butcher, Onofrio Buonocore, had proposed marriage, and she'd said no three times before she finally capitulated. I have their framed wedding picture still. In it, their witnesses flank them: my affable Uncle Nunzio and his wife, Auntie Marianina, four-foot-ten and as portly and droopy-breasted as the Venus of Willendorf. The groom puffs out his chest and beams like a conquering hero. The bride faces the camera stone-faced.

As for me, I continued my work for the WPA and later enrolled at Columbia University, where I earned a postgraduate degree in curatorial administration. Forever wary of the way in which one's art can tamper with one's sanity, I was, and remain, both an artist and a practical man. Our sons grew, thrived, and became Frankie, Stan, and Joey—bona fide New York kids who loved stickball, egg creams, and the Brooklyn Dodgers. Our boys, thank the Lord above, were still a few years too young to don uniforms and fight the Axis powers. Joey was the only one of the three who was at Nunzio's store the day Pee Wee Reese and Roy Campanella strolled in, bought peaches, and autographed the paper bag, which Joey later had me frame. From that day to this—the triplets are nearly fifty now!—he has lorded it over his disgruntled brothers: his close encounter with two of the greatest Dodgers ever.

In 1952, Anja, the boys, and I relocated to Connecticut, where I had been hired as director of the Statler Museum on the campus of the Three Rivers Academy. Since then, running the museum and hanging shows in its gallery hall is what has paid our bills and financed the college educations of Frank (a dermatologist), Stan (a geologist), and Joe (a television producer). But painting remained and still remains my primary calling. My work has been exhibited at the Corcoran Gallery, the Whitney, the Museum of Modern Art, and, I am proud to say, Chicago's Institute of Art. In 1977, one of my paintings was purchased for the Smithsonian Institute's permanent collection.

My Anja's heart stopped in 1986 and, after a paralyzing period of grief, I began again to enjoy the company of women—widows, mostly, although not exclusively. But I have not remarried. In old age, my canvas has become my wife. Or maybe this was always so. Daily, I sit before my easel and paint. Sometimes I work on a piece for weeks without knowing what I'm searching for, or for that matter, after I've finished it, what finally has been resolved. I only know that, to this day, little Fanny, my jump-roping muse, haunts and inspires me. I have painted her hundreds of times, in hundreds of ways. And strangely enough, each of these renderings—each brushstroke, really—carries me back to my papa, his art, and his *passione*.

NICHOLAS SAMARAS
I Like to Live with Hermits

Let me practice silence with you.

You have an extra room in your hut
and a wooden balcony overlooking a ravine of moonlight.

I can sleep in this bare corner, on the floor-planks
with a blanket and a stone for a pillow.

We can work on our separate projects in each other's shadow.

Let us develop telepathy, and I will hand you pepper for your soup
without looking up.

We could chant together only in Vespers, and separate
afterward into the gloom.

Let me sit on this rickety balcony, while silver rain falls, the blue air
gone wispy with another century.

Let me live in this corner and you won't notice me.

Let me be the ghost with eyes, tonsured with the wordless.

Let me practice stillness with you.

Neither of us here.

ANN LEARY
Safety

A hornet's nest hung above one of the French doors that led to the Quists' back terrace. Harrison Quist first noticed it when he took out the garbage one Thursday morning in early June. He told his wife, Marcie, about it as he dressed for work, calling it a bee's nest, and telling her to get somebody to come spray it that evening, after dark, when all the bees would have returned to their hive. "Get Bucky Porter to come do it," he said on his way out the door. "Get one of Bucky's guys."

Marcie didn't call Bucky Porter, not only because of her intense dislike for certain men on Bucky's crew, but also because she believed that she and Harrison should at least try to be involved in the maintenance of the house and property themselves. She felt that it set an example of some sort for their boys. She didn't wait until dark, as Harrison had suggested, because her father had always said that dusk was the best time to kill bees. It was a habit of Marcie's to measure her dead father against her living husband whenever it came to decisions regarding things to do with nature, or danger, or manliness in general, and her father always came out on top. Dusk was the best time to kill bees, according to Frank Barnes, who had been Westover's beloved high school football coach and who always knew the safest way to do things that weren't safe. So Marcie wandered out while it was still a little light, after the boys had finished their supper, while they sat watching television, drowsy and slightly damp from their afternoon at the beach and their baths. She stepped out onto the terrace with the spray can of insecticide, gazed up, and there, just above the door, was the nest.

It seemed to Marcie to be a perfect thing, this nest. It was pale silver and shaped like a round paper lantern with a series of smooth, raised ridges that were wrapped around the swollen structure in latitudinal swirls. Its outer shell was a thin, lacelike membrane, so fragile—*so fragile*—she kept thinking later, and they were hornets, not bees as Harrison had said.

She watched the detailed work that was being performed on the nest's opening, which was at the bottom, like the entrance to a womb. The hornets were using their black forelegs and pincers to delicately tweak the portal into a perfect O. They moved like a team of frantic fluttering surgeons, performing a sensitive operation on the nest, and the longer Marcie watched, the more the intricate structure appeared to pulse with life next to the rigid clapboards of their house. Hornets were floating above the nest in what appeared to be a patient holding pattern in the dying light of the afternoon, and Marcie wondered why they were so intent on their craftsmanship. Why did the nest have to be so perfectly symmetrical? Why was the portal a carefully honed circle rather than a ragged hole? She aimed the nozzle of the spray can at the last drones moving in and out of the nest, but she couldn't bring herself to spray them. They had been working so hard. And they weren't bothering anybody, not even she, who held an aerosol can of mass destruction in her hand, just inches from their world. She watched until it was almost dark and the air around the nest was finally still; then she stepped back into the house, closing the door carefully behind her.

The next day, six-year-old Alex Quist was stung five times on the head when he tried to enter the house through the patio door. One of his eyes was so swollen he could hardly open it, and Marcie had to rush him to the hospital. When she and Alex returned home, hours later, Harrison had sprayed the hornet's nest with Raid, then turned the jet stream of the garden hose on it until there was nothing left but gray clumps that dotted the lawn like bits of wet newspaper.

"Why the hell didn't you have Bucky Porter come out and spray it like I told you to?" Harrison shouted at his wife. He was wearing several layers of thick clothing and a hockey mask, and he was kicking at a piece of nest with the toe of his shoe. He now dropped the hose as he stomped on the last floundering, flightless hornets.

"I don't know. They were working so hard," Marcie said. She could still hear the droning sound, the dry song of the hornets. She glanced up as if she expected to see them swarming vindictively above her and she flinched several times, even though there was nothing there. Alex, woozy from suffering and antihistamines, was leaning against her leg. He squinted up at the towering silhouette of his father that was stomping and spinning in the painful afternoon sun.

"Dad?" he said.

"Well, ants work hard too," Harrison shot back, "but if we didn't have the exterminator come spray the house every month they'd be crawling all over us."

"Dad?" said his son.

Marcie shielded her eyes with a shaky hand and looked at her husband. The goalie's mask, which belonged to Alex, was slightly askew, so that one eye appeared higher than the other. Harrison looked like a child. He looked like a maniac.

"You know, a hornet could have gone right into one of those eyeholes," Marcie whispered. "There could be one crawling around in that mask right now." She turned as her husband cursed and whipped off the mask, then she followed her son into the house.

Harrison hosed the last bits of nest off the lawn. When he entered their kitchen, he saw that Marcie had poured beer into two tall glass mugs. The beer had been poured expertly, the foam crowning up over the top of the frosted glasses in perfect frothy domes. Marcie handed him one of the mugs. Her eyes were puffy from crying but now she took a sip of her beer. When she looked up at him, she managed to smile.

"Thanks," said Harrison, and he smiled back. Harrison sipped his beer and leaned back against the kitchen counter. "Sorry I yelled."

"No, you were right," she said, and then she was crying again. "Alex could have died. The doctor said he could have gone into anaphylactic shock—he's never been stung before, what if he was allergic?"

Harrison shot a look at the boys, who were watching TV in the den. "He wasn't going to die," Harrison insisted. "He's not allergic to bees, he's fine."

Marcie faced away from him. He stepped behind her and wrapped her in his arms and kissed the back of her neck, but she stiffened and after a moment, he moved away.

"Are we having your famous lasagna?" he asked.

"No, it's for the kids. We have that party at Wendy's tonight."

"No, not tonight. That's tonight? Let's skip it."

"We have to go. It's for some rich clients of hers. The Winthrops. The *wonderful* Winthrops," Marcie said. She took a long sip from her beer. "It'll be fine."

The sitter arrived at seven and Marcie gave her instructions about Alex's Benadryl and Tylenol and about the boys' TV allotment and bedtimes, and then she and Harrison drove off in their Volvo for the party at Wendy Heatherton's.

"Who are these people, these new *wonderfuls?*" asked Harrison as they pulled into the Heathertons' driveway.

"He's an investment banker, I think," said Marcie. "I guess they're young. They have a little baby. I'm not really sure."

Wendy Heatherton and Marcie had both grown up in Westover and had been friends since they were little girls. Wendy went to work as a receptionist at a local realtor's office upon graduation, and Marcie went to NYU on a track scholarship. Marcie's father had died suddenly of a heart attack the year before, and she had always been at odds with her fearful, fragile mother. She told her friends she would never return to her hometown, once she left, it was just too "provincial" for her, but when she did return, following her sophomore year, she was a borderline anorexic and a chain-smoker, and at the end of the summer, she stayed in Westover instead of returning to school. She needed to care for her mother, she said, and besides, her boyfriend, Harrison, whom she'd met on a train, was at Harvard Law School.

Marcie's mother died not long after Harrison joined a large Boston firm, and Wendy helped them sell the house on Hat Shop Hill Road where the old woman had spent her final years hoarding cats and bottles and garbage and peering out of the windows in horror whenever a car pulled up, like a witch hiding from the cruelly pious. Then they bought the Fullerton house up on Painter's Ridge, overlooking the harbor, because Harrison had made junior partner and Marcie had forgotten why it was she never wanted to return to her hometown. She had quit smoking and gained some of the youthful plumpness around her face. She had a son by then and another on the way.

"Why does Wendy have to *clasp* everybody with those man-hands of hers," Harrison mumbled to Marcie as they climbed the steps to Wendy's house.

"What? What do you mean *clasp?*"

"She doesn't just shake your hand or hug you, she clasps your hand and won't let go. You never noticed that?"

"No," Marcie laughed. "Maybe she just does it to men. Maybe it's just you."

Marcie was wearing a new summer dress. She had placed cucumber slices over her eyes and the puffiness had gone down, and now she felt rather pretty and she reached for her husband's hand. The door swung open and a young woman, one of the caterer's girls, welcomed them into the house and showed them out to the patio.

Wendy Heatherton always liked to throw a party for clients of hers that she thought were "wonderful." It was her way of thanking them for buying a home from her, and also a way to introduce them to the other "wonderful" people in the community. There was always a bar set up in the corner of her patio at these parties, and it was always Rick Tucker from the meat counter at the Westover Market who worked the bar. Marcie smiled when she saw Rick, but as she and Harrison made their way over, Wendy was suddenly upon them.

"There you are Marcie, Harrison!" She took turns sandwiching each of their hands between hers. "You're just in time, we're about to sit down to dinner, but first, come. Come meet our wonderful new neighbors, the Winthrops."

"I'm going to get us a drink," said Marcie, glancing down at Harrison's hand that was still clasped in Wendy's. Wendy's hands were enormous. Marcie had never noticed. Harrison rolled his eyes and Marcie laughed with him as Wendy led him away.

It was one of the first warm nights of summer and the small party seemed to have already found its momentum. "There she is!" exclaimed David Weiss, whose daughter, Lily, was in Alex's class. He was standing next to the bar and when Marcie went to kiss his cheek he grabbed her about the waist in a rough hug. Marcie realized that the cocktails must have started earlier than she had thought. She had forgotten to check the invitation that day in all the confusion. The Ryans were there, the Klemms, the Tittmans. The Venezuelans who bought the old Barrow property out on Stead's Point. Westover was a small town and recent settlers were always eager to meet newer arrivals. Marcie and Wendy were usually the only real Westover natives at these welcoming parties, besides the caterers and bartenders. The others were people who'd been drawn to the beauty of the New England coastal town, the quaint architecture, all the history and lore. As Marcie watched Wendy lead Harrison over to the group surrounding the newly arrived Winthrops, she ordered a vodka and cranberry from Rick.

"Cape Coddah, I know," Rick laughed. He worked most of the parties in Westover. "What about Harrison? A Heinie?"

"Sure, thanks Rick."

By the time they all sat down to dinner in Wendy's dining room, Marcie had finished a second cocktail, and she smiled at Brad Winthrop, who was seated next to her, and answered his questions about the town.

"It's a nice place to grow up," she said, recalling for him her summers riding her bike around town, playing at the town beaches and learning to sail.

"Where did you grow up?" asked Brad.

"On Hat Shop Hill, it's a road that leads into town."

"Is that where you live now?" Brad asked her.

From the far end of the table, Marcie heard Harrison telling his bee story.

"It was like one of those cartoons! Three thousand fucking bees formed a giant arrow pointing right at my head…" His words were drowned by the laughter of those seated around him.

"No, we're up on Painter's Ridge," Marcie said to Brad.

"That's right, Wendy showed us your place once. The cottage with those amazing views of the harbor. That's a beautiful spot."

"Next time we'll get Bucky up there to battle the wildlife," boomed Harrison from his end of the table.

Marcie bristled at the sound of her husband dropping Bruce Porter's nickname, "Bucky." His tendency to do this, to refer to local tradesmen—all former schoolmates of Marcie's—with a breezy familiarity that implied a oneness with the working man, infuriated Marcie.

As if they were old drinking buddies.

In fact, Bucky Porter thought Harrison's name was Garrison.

In fact, Bucky Porter had been Marcie's boyfriend. She was tempted, from time to time, to tell Harrison about how she and Bucky used to borrow the Anawam Yacht Club's launch, late at night, the summer after her sophomore year in high school. Marcie waitressed at the club and Bucky worked on some of the members' boats and he knew where they all kept their booze. She and Bucky would sit on the splendid bows of the gently rocking boats and drink wine straight from the bottle and blink up at the stars. They'd smoke a joint and make out. On hot nights, when they were drunk enough, they'd undress and swim. One night, on a sleek wood-hulled yacht, after the kissing, she followed him down into the boat's dark hold. He was her first. They had jammed themselves into a slim cushioned berth and covered each other with hot, wet, open-mouthed kisses. Water sloshed against the outside of the hull. Love was so urgent and dangerous then, and that lovely dull pain of first sex that lasted for days had made her heart tumble and pulse. It was like a cartoon heart; Marcie thought people might actually be able to see it pounding away under her skin whenever she thought of Bucky Porter that summer. He had been handsome in those days, in a rough sort of way. She looked down the table and saw Harrison high-fiving Gina Brighanti and then guffawing with her over something she had said. Marcie turned her attention back to Brad.

"It must be odd to see the house you grew up in with other people living in it," he was saying.

"Actually, the people who bought it tore it down. They built another house. A sort of McMansion, I guess you'd call it."

"Oh, I'm sorry…"

"No, it's fine," Wendy said, smiling up at him. This was what Marcie loved about new people—their ability to see Westover only as it existed now; with all the other new "wonderfuls" restoring homes, joining the historic commission, and working hard to keep Westover the way they thought it had always been. It was likely Brad Winthrop envisioned her childhood home as a charming antique with a cobblestone path and a cat in a window, *one cat,* peering out from behind a lace curtain, not the place of disarray and drunken sorrow that had contained her mother for so many years.

When dessert was served, Brad's wife, Jill, moved over to sit beside him, and Marcie filled her in on all the best babysitters and the best places in town to buy produce and fish. She warned them of the dangerous riptides at North Beach. A local teenager named Molly was circling the table with bottles of red and white wine, absent-mindedly refilling empty wine glasses. Marcie recalled doing the same thing when she had been hired to work at parties as a teenager. She knew that her adult voice and the others' were just a dull droning to the pretty young girl who was probably lost in thoughts of the coming year, when she would be gone from Westover, and from all of them. When Marcie asked Molly for more red, the girl started pouring white and Marcie said, "Just leave the bottles on the table, Molly, you're making us dizzy with all your circling back and forth."

Marcie had been having trouble sleeping ever since the birth of her younger son Ben, and the morning after Wendy's party, she woke up before dawn. Her head ached dully from the wine she had drunk at the party and she was gripped with anxiety—about the boys, about money, about things she had said to Harrison on the way home from the party. She had mocked him for his fabricated bravado about the bees, which, she informed him again, were not even bees. "Hornets! They were fucking hornets! There's a difference!" He had told her she'd better watch her drinking or she'd wind up a drunk like her mother, a "pathetic drunk" he had said, and she went back to sleep in the attic, which they had converted into a tiny office with a guest bed. She woke up to the sound of a small animal scratching about in the wall next to her head.

The psychotherapist that Marcie had recently begun seeing had encouraged her to get out of bed instead of devoting those predawn hours to self-recrimination, and she decided that it would be a good morning to plant some of the annuals that she'd bought earlier in the week. She had placed the flats of red impatiens in the shade of a centuries-old maple tree that loomed over the back garden, and now she wandered out in the waning darkness and began moving them, one by one, over to the beds surrounding her terrace. Each flat contained a dozen seedlings. She found a spade and a heavy bag of potting soil in the garage and carried them outside. She still wore her white cotton nightgown and her intention had been to change into clothes once she had all the gardening supplies assembled, but when she saw the seedlings gathered there in such neat expectant rows, she was so overcome with the urge to begin planting that she knelt and plunged her spade into last year's hardened dirt.

By the time Marcie had flung the first empty plastic seedling tray onto the lawn, the night had dissolved into dawn. The Quists' house was located above a rocky ledge that overlooked Westover Harbor, and Marcie gazed down at the wharf where the shops and the town landing were beginning to take their shape. She spied old Manny Briggs loading empty traps onto his lobster boat, *Mercy*. Manny was wearing the yellow oilskin overalls that are the lobsterman's uniform even on the hottest summer days. It was that moment of day on the waterfront when the sky and sea took on the exact same shade of gray and the horizon was lost. There was just a boat and a dock, seeming to float in air, with Manny in bright cautionary yellow, moving back and forth between them. The clanging of the traps against the boat's hull, the chugging of the engine, and the mournful cry of gulls filled Marcie with the aching sadness that had made it so difficult to eat and to sleep lately. Why had she ever come back to Westover? She still missed her father and loathed her poor dead mother. She was a terrible mother to her boys, an ungrateful wife. She scraped away at the hard ground, her head pounding.

Harrison found her on the way out to his car, two hours later. Her nightgown was covered with soil and her face was streaked with sweat and dirt. She had planted several flats of impatiens. When Harrison commented on the earliness of the hour, Marcie wiped her hair from her eyes with a forearm and asked him if the boys were up.

"Just Ben," Harrison answered. "He's watching cartoons. It's OK. He's fine. It's still early."

"Is it? OK." Marcie said.

Harrison noticed a large pair of hedgerow clippers that lay next to Marcie's bare feet. "What are you doing with these?"

"The hedges." said Marcie. "You said you were going to trim the hedges but you never did, so I'm going to do them after I take the boys to day camp."

"I called Bucky about that. He'll send somebody over later this morning. Don't mess around with those clippers."

"You called Bucky to do the hedges? Do you know how much he charges?"

Harrison threw his briefcase in the back of his car. "We can afford it," he said.

When he backed down the gravel drive and sped off, Marcie planted a few more impatiens, and then she decided that she would get dressed and trim the hedges before Bucky arrived. She planned to send him on his way the minute he pulled up. There were plenty of other people who needed Bucky in town. Plenty. His own wife, for one, their place was a mess.

She would just plant a few more. The bed was almost done. She was easing a seedling from its tray when she heard the crush of gravel from the driveway. She recognized the sound of Bucky's rusty old diesel-engine pickup but she didn't even look up. Instead she cut another hole into the last hard crumble, the final unplanted corner of the flowerbed. She dropped the spade, scooped a handful of topsoil from the bag, and then pressed the soil into the hole. She tapped the roots of a little plant against her bare knee to knock off some of the old dirt, to help free up the roots that had been so tightly bound, and then, carefully holding its slender stem between two fingers, she set it in the hole, tamping the fresh soil all around it until it stood, wavering slightly, slim-necked and flat-headed, all by itself.

"Jesus, Marcie," Bucky said. He was standing on the terrace surveying her work. "You planted all these this morning?"

"Yeah, and I'm doing the hedges too, Buck. You don't need to stay. I don't know why Harrison called you."

Bucky squatted next to the flowerbed and tipped one of the last plants from its tray. Then he reached into the soil with his free hand; Marcie's cool fingers were moving through the soft loam like smooth, slender worms, and he covered them with his hand. She smiled and tangled her fingers playfully in his for a moment, but when he pressed his lips to her neck, she wriggled free.

"The kids," she whispered, nodding at the house.

"Don't they have camp today?" he said, standing up. "I thought they'd started camp."

"I'm taking them at nine," Marcie said. "I'll be back by 9:30."

Marcie's toes were covered in loose dirt. Bucky started gathering the empty trays. From the house behind them came the chaotic clamor of television cartoons.

"Hand me the clippers, Marce," Bucky said. "I'll get those hedges started."

Marcie handed them to him the way her father had taught her, with the sharp points held together in her two hands for safety. Then she placed the last plant in its tiny plot and sat back on her heels. There they were, all the little impatiens—the flush of blood-red singletons—radiating out and all around her in brilliant concentric rows. Her day took shape for her then. She would shower and take her boys to camp. She would call her husband to apologize for last night and to tell him that Bucky was there. Bucky had come to do the hedges, they were all safe. She wiped the soil from her palms and when Bucky leaned over and offered her his rough familiar hand, she took it and he plucked her from the center of the flowerbed and placed her on the lawn, then he held her for a moment while she steadied herself.

PHILIP SCHULTZ
Hitting and Getting Hit

They could say what they liked,
imitate the way I stuttered
the morning Pledge, mashed
the alphabet, ask how many
chickens 1 plus 3 made, why
my brain sat in a corner, in a class
of one, refused to read or write,
was nailed to my tongue, just as long
as they understood that some
with my fist would be kissed,
yanked off bikes by their hair,
their eyeballs thumb-scrubbed,
faces autographed by sidewalks,
that under no circumstances would
they ever make me cry. In newsreels
Dad and I watched withered souls
in striped pajamas stare from
behind electrified wire, as if not seeing
or asking why would save them.
Jews like us, Dad said. The next day
he threw a man twice his size down
factory stairs because he didn't say
good morning back. I understood then
that dignity wasn't an entitlement,
goodness didn't mean being good,
justice wouldn't be my inheritance.
Even after the Hildebrand twins hung
me upside down from deaf Mrs. Polowska's
cherry tree, pushed me off their garage roof
through crazy Mr. Selby's porch window,
who then chased us with a pitchfork,

a Red Sea squirting from my thumb,
Mom screaming at God for hating us,
Benny the junkman driving me to the ER
in his souped-up Dodge pickup, where
the doc asked, Isn't this the third time
I've stitched you up? I wouldn't. Not even
when a Wop and two Polacks wrote *kike*
in black lipstick on my forehead, kicked me
in the stomach five times, because in our
neighborhood Jews paid to go to school,
and I sat drinking Cokes and spitting blood
in our uncut backyard grass and then went
looking for them and cops picked me up
and drove me around, explaining the way
things worked: Know who to be afraid of, son.
Not even after I didn't go to school and snuck
into the Paramount to sit in the filthy dark grid
of the balcony, stinking of popcorn and savoring
every eschatological thought the rowdy cowboys
and impenitent gangsters mumbled about how
freedom, privacy, and mercy were expendable
if you owned enough land oil cattle and violence,
enough pilgrim faith in belonging somewhere.
Not even up there, under the painted stars,
with only an illiterate God for company, surrounded
by the ear-popping serendipity of the swooning music,
even after understanding that fitting in was what
Dad wanted too, and the withered souls,
to be Poles, French, and German, to belong to
the ever-westward expanding magnificence
of some manifest destiny, no matter how impossible,
and the harm done to oneself and others—why
every morning we sat at the kitchen table
steeped in grief and irresistible hunger, hating
our coffee, cereal, and broken minds, watching
snow fall over every tired tree, house, and hour

of our utter bewilderment, believing nothing
worked out, waiting for an always late, beaten-
to-a-pulp truth to arrive, until one January morning
I suddenly started crying and never stopped.

MEGAN SEXTON
Ode to Silence

Glory to the half rest, to the breath between
    the third and fourth beats,
        the dwindling arrow of the decrescendo,

to the sunrise over Malibu, and its sleeping starlets,
    the empty horizon,
        the city's great thought still looming,

to parked cars, the cold engine seconds before ignition
    dreaming of the road
        unwound and endless,

to the lull before ecstasy, the saint's vigil
    of the dark soul in suffering,
        the grip of the heart before release,

to the inaction of love before the reaction,
    of the hand before it reaches out,
        its sharp twitch of self-consciousness,

to the embryo, the soft dream of the womb,
    the golden truth of genesis,
        the sustained hush and its amplitude.

FIRST ANNUAL EMERGING FICTION WRITER'S CONTEST WINNER

THOMAS LEE
The Gospel of Blackbird

As John hurried to the resident locker room after doing his rounds at Columbia Presbyterian Hospital, he noticed a sixtyish Korean lady in red sweats cautiously stalking him from about twenty feet away. At first, John thought the wrinkled woman might be a figment of his overworked brain, as he was always tired to the point of incoherence and often talked to himself during the second year of his surgical residency. He hated his daily demands so much he wouldn't have been surprised if hallucinations were the next step in his unraveling.

The old woman had permed hair that resembled rusty poodle fur and a withered overpowdered face that reminded John of a kabuki performer. When John turned away from his ghastly stalker and walked down the hallway, she ran toward him and poked his shoulder.

"Don't you bow to your elders?" she asked in Korean as he turned. Although his parents had tried to teach him Korean in his youth, John barely understood that simple sentence, as the language didn't stick to him in the Long Island suburbs.

"I'm sorry. I don't think I know you," he said hesitantly in English and turned again, trying to skirt the intrusive questions Koreans often ask other Koreans.

"I'm Na-Jin's mother. Remember? Nancy?"

John's eyes widened, as if he'd just been injected with adrenaline. He had tried to forget Nancy many times over the years, but had not succeeded, often replaying scenes from their short time together while he lay alone in his Washington Heights studio.

The old woman smiled. "You remember her. You loved her."

She started speaking Korean in a blistering pace. He couldn't keep up with the woman's verbal torrent, with only certain familiar words that his parents sometimes used jumping out at him. "Church...Cancer...God...Boy...Queens."

He raised his palms and shrugged. Frustrated, she clutched a tarnished silver crucifix that she wore around her neck. She said slowly in English, like a toddler speaking, "Nancy will die. I need help. For Nancy. A boy talks to God. He can help her. Make her better."

John's insides shivered when she said "die," but he shook his head, afraid of how Nancy might affect his life again. In broken Korean, he then explained, "A boy? God? I don't understand you. I can't help."

"Your Korean is bad," she groaned. In his parents' minds, John more than made up for that critical flaw by going to medical school at their behest.

She shook her head, and then said, "I'll write you a letter. For you to give to your mother. Stay here and don't move." Because she was twice his age and Korean, John did as he was told.

One of the hospital's nurses, a husky blond woman who wore librarian glasses, came by and asked, "What does she want from you?"

"She's going to write a letter to my mother."

The nurse said with a furrowed brow, "She's a very strange woman. Her daughter has leukemia, which looks real bad. The nurses in the cancer ward say she brings in nut jobs during visiting hours."

"She asked me about a boy who can heal her daughter," John said.

"Doesn't surprise me. These people who came by with her last week did loud chants for like an hour."

"Korean people?"

The nurse said, "They were Asian. And the way they prayed was scary. Crying and screaming with their hands in the air. I'd be careful with her."

The nurse marched away as the Korean woman came by again holding a letter written on loose-leaf paper. John could not read Korean, so it was just a jumble of quirky symbols to him.

"Give that to your mother. She will know what it means," Nancy's mom said.

One December Sunday twelve years before, John was arranging folding chairs in the teen service room of the largest Korean church in suburban Long Island, where John's father was the minister. John, though seventeen and yearning to be free of filial obligations, always had to come early to help the youth pastor set up. That day, five minutes before the service, Nancy strode in, her tiny body propped by platform heels clopping against the linoleum floor. She instantly drew stares and whispers from the other teens gathered in the windowless classroom. She was as small as an elementary school girl, but wore twice as much makeup as any church mother, and dyed her hair jet-black with purple streaks. Wearing drugstore aviator sunglasses and layers of black under a black trench coat, she looked to John like she had dressed for a vampire's funeral.

John approached her as she stood alone in the back of the room staring blankly into the yellow plaster wall. He usually sat somewhere near the front, so he could lead youth group prayers, but he instinctively wanted to be next to the only girl at church who had ever intrigued him.

"Are you new here?" he asked. Just over six feet, he was a foot taller than she was.

"Yeah. I already know who you are though," she smirked.

Every Korean parent in a sixty-mile radius revered and envied his gray-maned father for raising a tall soccer star with stellar grades. No one knew that John hated being a poster child for the greater New York Korean American second generation, and wanted nothing more than a momentary escape.

"You mind if I sit with you? I'm supposed to welcome the newbies." He smiled, hoping that didn't sound too dorky.

"Do whatever. My mom made me come here," she said.

"Mine too. Every week since birth," he said, making her grin just a bit.

The chubby, twenty-something youth minister stood up in front to address the forty Korean boys and girls dressed almost uniformly in white button-down tops and black slacks. "We have a new person with us today. Nancy Jung, can you please stand up?"

"Oh God," she muttered under her breath as she rose.

"Um, I'm sorry but could you take off your sunglasses, please?" the dough-boy minister said.

She stood motionless.

"This is a place of worship. It's just a little disrespectful."

She shrugged and swiped off her glasses, revealing artificial ice-blue irises. The youth minister's brown eyes bulged behind his thick glasses. He shook his head, looked at the rest of the congregation and said, "OK, let's start with a prayer..."

After the service began, Nancy looked down at her yellow Swatch every five minutes. John glanced at her repeatedly, attracted to the cherubic, teddy-bearish features underneath all her dark camouflage.

The other teenagers in the room sang praise songs, making hand gestures in unison with the lyrics. "From the rising of the sun..." They raised their hands skyward with eyes closed, cupping an imaginary sun without even a hint of cynicism. John viewed the service with an outsider's eyes for the first time and thought the congregation must've looked like a cult of lemmings to a girl as rebellious as Nancy.

"Why aren't you doing it?" Nancy whispered as John slouched in his seat.

"Cuz it's totally gay," he whispered back. She chuckled with surprise, causing a few heads to turn in their direction.

"You wanna cut out?" Nancy dared.

"Yeah," he said, trying to seem nonchalant though his heart rate accelerated, as he had never done anything more than hold a girl's hand before.

"Say you gotta go to the bathroom. I'll meet you outside in five minutes," Nancy said.

After they met at the church entrance on that chilly morning, they walked a couple of blocks into the main street of brick single-story storefronts. John bought gummy worms from the 7-Eleven, which they ate as they sat on the curb, their breath visible in the winter air.

"Isn't a minister's son scared of hell?" she asked.

"Not any more than you are," John said with a shrug.

Nancy explained that her daddy was a drunk who went back to Korea when she was four. She bounced around with her mom, who spoke almost no English, to wherever some Korean business was willing to hire cheap help. Her last stop was outside Dallas, where her mom worked in a nail salon while Nancy hung out in trailer parks with a druggie crowd. A few months back, her mom was laid off, but found a job at a restaurant supply store on Long Island through a family friend, and moved to a one-bedroom atop a stinky fish market in Queens.

"I thought everyone would look at me like I was trash here, but you're kinda cool. So far, anyway." She flashed an inviting smile.

"Cool." John had rarely heard anyone use that word to describe him. Because his family always forced him onto the straight path, he never qualified for his suburban high school's social elite, narcotized preppy slackers orphaned by professional parents. Korean kids respected him, but were always uncomfortably proper around him.

"Follow me," she said, her fake eyes sparkling. She led him to a gray Honda Civic in the church parking lot, took a set of keys out of her little black leather purse, and opened the back door. John's pulse doubled, and his hands involuntarily clenched into fists.

"Done this before?" she asked, giggling.

John paused for a moment, thinking of his father giving a sermon just yards away, but then looked at Nancy's mischievous eyes and said, his voice an octave higher than normal, "Yeah, this is cool."

John kissed with his mouth open for the first time as they clumsily fumbled with each other in the backseat. She was so petite that John could cover her entire ribcage with his open right hand. When he moved his hand farther upward, he felt just a palmful more than a boy's chest, but began to breathe heavily. She unbuttoned his dress shirt and put her tiny hands inside, sending a crackling electric current over his lightly muscled chest.

She had moved her right hand into his trousers when, suddenly, the chubby youth pastor knocked on the back window. Seeing Nancy with her hand in John's crotch, the rotund young man of God simply shook his head with disgust.

"I'm talking to your mothers," he screamed through the closed window.

"What are you gonna do? Kick me out of Sunday School?" she mocked, delighting in defiling the minister's son. She beamed with pride at her achievement.

After he drove the family home from church, John's father slammed the door to the master bedroom and refused to come out. John was quite happy to not have to listen to another one of his father's sanctimonious lectures on how Koreans were one of the most Christian people in the world, and a Korean boy's duty was obedience to the Scriptures.

His mother walked into his room that night, looking disappointed but concerned behind her horn-rimmed spectacles. Although a perpetually harried businesswoman who only had a few hours a week for John, she always tempered his father's wrath with rational counseling.

"Why did you do this, John?" she asked.

"Just sick of being a savior," John said, plopping down on his bed.

His mother glared downward at him. Nearly as tall as John, she straightened herself to her full height when she wanted to make a point. "You have no idea how lucky you are, John. Nancy's a troubled girl and I hope God saves her one day, but she can ruin you. You don't know it now, but believe me, you need to be careful."

"Maybe I wouldn't mind being ruined," John retorted.

"Think about what you're saying, John. Think about your family," his mom said before she left the room.

In the weeks that followed, when he encountered Koreans at the mall or supermarket, he could see them whisper to each other, "The minister's son. Can you believe it?" He was exhilarated by his first taste of scandal.

After John completed his rounds at the hospital, he took the 1-9 downtown to the crowded sidewalks of 32nd street and, as ordered by Nancy's mother, brought the letter to his mom in her disheveled cubicle in a twenty-story office building near Koreatown. For the last twenty-five years, she had been a real estate agent who led the relatively well-to-do Koreans out of Queens and into well-groomed suburban zones that WASPs were abandoning. To John's bemusement, his father preached that a woman's role was subservience to her husband, even though his own wife could buy and sell him.

When John arrived, his mother was pulling at her bob cut as she fluttered in a wrinkled Talbot's suit over piles of manila folders. "I don't have much time. What is it?" she asked.

John showed her the handwritten letter, "Nancy's mother found me at the hospital. She told me to give this to you."

"Nancy? That girl? From when you were in high school?"

"Yes."

His mother scanned the letter with pursed lips. "Nancy has cancer. There's some boy that can cure her. Apparently, he's cured a few other cancer patients. Many of the Korean churches out in Queens seem to believe he's a miracle boy."

"Miracle? Like a faith healer?"

"Yes, he has wounds like Jesus. He bleeds like him. His touch will make her better."

"That's insane."

"I know. Someone is taking advantage of this poor woman. She's been through enough."

"What does she want from me?"

His mother didn't answer until she reached the end of the letter. "She wants to know if you, a doctor, had heard of anyone being cured like this in New York. She wants to know if this is real, and if you can tell if she's cured afterward."

"Doesn't she have doctors?"

"They're probably not Korean. They wouldn't understand something like this."

"I don't understand this, Mom. This is crazy." John was raised to believe in God's miracles, but, as a doctor, he considered faith healers nothing more than despicable predators. He wanted to suspend his skepticism for Nancy's sake, but was not sure if he could.

"You should help her, John." His mom focused her gaze on her confused son.

"How?"

"Go with them. Be her doctor through this. Tell her what she should believe in."

"You told me to stay away from her, Mom."

"I also told you about God's grace, John. It's been years," his mother said.

John's mother didn't know how much he'd seen Nancy after the incident at church. Three days after getting caught in the car with her, he called down the list of Jungs in the church address book when his parents were away at a prayer meeting, until a heavily accented voice said "OK" when he asked for Nancy.

"I'm still not afraid of hell. You?" he said when she answered.

Nancy chuckled, "Very cool of you to call."

In the few months he had before Yale, he would sneak out to the mall to meet Nancy before his parents got home, or steal a quick hour or two with her in one of their living rooms. The next fall, she occasionally visited him in New Haven. She didn't go to college, deciding instead to traverse through lower Manhattan, bouncing around random couches and beds, sometimes finding her way back home to Queens to her crying mother. Something was always missing from his dorm room when she left, a few dollar bills he had left on his dresser, change for the laundry, and, once, his digital watch. He learned to hide his wallet deep in his sweater drawer when she came by.

For the next couple of years, he eagerly awaited her two or three visits a semester, even though he sensed she was using him as a quick respite from a helter-skelter life in New York. John tried to get along with other girls at school, but he bored the ones he liked, and the ones who liked him were boring. In the end, none of them could take his mind off Nancy. She'd call a day or two in advance and show up at the Metro North station with a dumpy overnight bag, looking disheveled and sad, but always donning her fake blue eyes.

One autumn day during his junior year, she took his keys and wandered around the Gothic steeples while he studied advanced biology in his room. She carried around his backpack, telling the boys that she might transfer to Yale from a small school down in Texas. She came back with many phone numbers, which she presented to John and laughed. "Total dorkwads."

"They're not all so bad," he responded.

"I don't know how you sit cooped up in this place." She shook her head at the hardcover science textbooks lying piled next to his bed.

"I have to if I'm gonna be a doctor," John answered.

"Do you even want to be a doctor?"

When John paused without an answer, she laughed. "You've never even asked yourself that, have you? You don't even know what you want to do."

"Maybe not yet. Do you know what you want?"

"Yeah. I'm gonna be a singer. I even have a name. You remember that nursery rhyme?" She started to sing in a delicate but tone-deaf soprano.

Four and twenty blackbirds,
Baked in a pie.
When the pie was opened,
The birds began to sing.

She giggled when she was done. "That's what I'm gonna call myself. Blackbird. Cuz they sing, stay true to themselves, even when they're about to be cut to pieces."

They ordered pizza, and slept together uncomfortably nestled in his concave dorm twin bed. As she slept, he tried to think of ways to get her to stay longer, perhaps offer to take her to some woodsy New England getaway, but when he awoke, she was gone.

The middle of the next week, he walked home dazed from midterms and found Nancy crumpled into a ball underneath the blue sheets of his twin bed, sweating like she had just finished a marathon. She had strewn all her clothes, including her white bra and panties, across his dusty wood floor. He shook her awake and all she said was, "I needed a place to crash."

"How'd you get in?" John demanded.

She pointed nonchalantly to two keys linked by a flimsy chain beside his cheap clock radio. John realized she had made copies at some point while she had roamed the campus.

"That's a Yale ID too," she said. A clumsily laminated card sat next to the keys.

John looked into her ice-blue eyes and saw that she couldn't focus them. "You on something?"

She shook her head.

"What happened?" John said, sitting down at his computer desk, which sat two feet from his twin bed in his sparse concrete dorm.

"My mom is threatening to put me away, all that crap. She wants to lock me up in some Jesus-freak death camp, but I'm twenty. Can do what I want now."

"Did she cut you off?"

"Yeah. I'll find a way though."

She smiled luridly as she sat up and pulled the blue sheet down to reveal her bare chest. John was not enticed as her eyes veered in two different directions, "I need a little money so I can get back to the city," she said.

"Here," he said. He pulled a twenty out of his wallet and handed it to her, though he felt awkward, like he was paying to see her naked.

"Can I get a little more? I wanna get my nails done. I'll pay you back, of course." Her nails looked like they had been gnawed by rodents.

John opened his wallet to give her another twenty and said, "I read in a magazine that there's a shampoo girls use, just for a few days, to cleanse themselves of the cooler ones they use every day. After that, the cool ones work better."

"Yeah, so?"

"I'm like that shampoo, huh?"

She chuckled, "Come on now, we're old friends, aren't we?"

"I'm not stupid. How many guys you got in New York? Older, I bet. Got money."

She didn't answer, just looked away and smiled. "If you're shampoo, what am I?"

John remembered his freshman Greek mythology class. "Do you know what a succubus is?"

She shook her head.

"It's a demon girl that steals a man's life force by sleeping with him. Sucks it in and makes herself stronger."

"Now you're just being stupid."

"Why do you keep coming here?"

She looked down at the floor. "Maybe I need you."

"I'm taking my keys back," John said as he grabbed them off the computer desk. He took her fake ID too.

"What's your problem? Why are you acting like you're my dad?" she shouted as she rose in disbelief. The sheets slipped off her and fell to the floor, leaving her aquiline body, marked with inflamed bruises on her skinny arms and ribs, completely exposed.

She glowered up at him, her azure eyes, now acutely focused, piercing the darkness of the room, "You think you know me, you stupid fuck? Well, I know you. You're just a lapdog looking for praise. I only said you were cool cuz I feel sorry for you. Who else is gonna think that of you but a bunch of old Koreans at church?"

Nancy's mother was waiting for John the next day, in the same spot next to the resident lockers where she had first tracked him down. John said in Korean that he had practiced with his mother, "I will help you. I will go with you and Nancy to the healer. We will see together if he is real."

The next day, two small women awaited him at that spot. As John walked down the hall, his eyes fixed on the younger one with dour natural brown eyes. Nancy now had just baby fuzz for hair, and hollow sullen cheeks. John eyeballed her terminal diagnosis and guessed that she had perhaps a few months left. Her pretty features weathered and whittled, she seemed too tired for defiance and smiled politely when she saw him. Her wool sweater and jeans drooped over her bones, so she resembled a child who had dressed herself from her mother's closet.

"You look the same. A little older, but the same," Nancy said. He nodded politely.

"Look, I didn't want to bother you. I'm doing this for my mom. Figure I put her through enough, so I should do as she says now," she shrugged. Although Nancy was the most vivid part of his young adulthood, John believed her memories of him were probably fading photos in a rarely opened album that contained many men from her past, soon to be gone forever.

"You don't hold a grudge?" Nancy asked.

"That was a long time ago." Truthfully, he had resented her, wincing with hurt pride when he remembered their last night together.

Nancy's mother led them toward the exit. John said as he walked with Nancy, "Your mom wants me to check you after this boy touches you. Honestly, I don't know what to expect. Do you believe in this boy?"

"Not really. But what have I got to lose?"

Nancy's mother guided them to a rusty red Nissan Stanza that looked as if it could barely struggle out of the hospital parking lot, much less transport them to some miracle. She opened the back door and, as if she were a chauffeur, motioned for John and Nancy to get inside.

Nestled shoulder-to-shoulder in the back, Nancy and John rode in silence for about five minutes until Nancy finally said, "I know things didn't end well, but I was in a really bad place then. You were my sanctuary."

About half an hour later, John saw that they were headed into the verdant lawns of Forest Hills. When Nancy's mom said they were going to Queens, he assumed she meant Flushing, where Koreans lived densely massed into noisy high-rises. Instead, they pulled into a ranch-style house situated on a maple-lined block that could serve as a backdrop for a family television show.

When Nancy's mom rang the doorbell, a bespectacled Korean man clad entirely in black appeared at the front door. Nancy's mom handed the man a stuffed envelope. A few hundred of those envelopes bought this respectable house of God, John thought.

Seven middle-aged Korean men in black priestly robes walked into the foyer, and marched them all into an unfurnished room with hardwood floors covered only with a large bamboo mat in the center. The men lined the back wall and motioned for Nancy, her mom and John to sit on the mat. For a while, the men muttered incomprehensible prayers in a low drone, their voices meshing into a buzz like a swarm of insects. Nancy and John shared a few uncomfortable glances while they quietly knelt, waiting to see whether these men really could produce a miracle.

After a few minutes, a stick-skinny boy a head shorter than Nancy and, at most, nine years old entered the room wearing a flowing white robe and sandals. Nancy and John both gasped when they saw him, as his bones jutted out from the thin material of his robe. With long, unruly hair matted against skin as translucent as rice paper, he looked like a scrawny cadaver that would fall apart if touched.

The only lively part of him was his wondrous eyes. They were enormous dark ovals enveloped with a sadness that belied his age, like dark wells where desperate souls had whispered their last wishes.

"He's the one who needs a healer," John said to Nancy.

"Shhhhhhh!" One of the men warned. He motioned for all in the room to pray, but John's eyes remained on the boy.

The boy approached Nancy. "Let him touch you," one of the men said in halting English.

Nancy's mother said a slew of sentences about the boy in Korean that John couldn't understand.

On the boy's palms, John noticed two-inch cuts covered by fresh scabs, likely puncture wounds from some sort of clumsy self-mutilation done with an object not sharp enough to penetrate deeply. The boy didn't bleed like Jesus, John thought. He bled because these men demanded it. As much as John wanted to see a supernatural connection, he knew a true sign from God would not be so sloppy.

Nancy said in English, "You're hurting him. Can't you see that? He's just a boy."

One of the men responded in a thick accent, "He will make you better."

"No. This is wrong. This is just a circus trick for money." Nancy looked around the room, her eyes tearing.

Nancy focused on John, pleading, "We can report them, can't we? We have to get him out of there."

John shook his head, despising the men for exploiting a boy in God's name, but knowing they were untouchable from outsiders. How many times had his father's church kept a pregnant teen, a battered spouse, or an illegal immigrant out of sight of anyone not Korean, to be dealt with covertly within their community, invisible to any other eyes?

"He's a scared little boy," Nancy said to John.

"It's no use," John replied with gritted teeth. "We can't help him." A cold dead weight grew in the pit of his stomach when he saw Nancy's eyes smolder with anger. Nancy's mom desperately looked skyward for a divine revelation.

"He's doing what they want him to. He's too scared not to," Nancy said.

John glared hatefully at all the stout, stern men standing around the room, knowing this boy would soon vanish, as if an impenetrable curtain had dropped around him.

"Leave him alone!" she screamed in Korean, rising from the mat.

The boy shuffled into a corner and covered his ears with his wounded hands.

The men approached, one of them putting a bear hug around Nancy while the others pushed her as a crowd toward the front door. John and Nancy's mom tried to push through the men to get to Nancy, but there were too many of them, and John found himself forced outside by a current of bodies.

After they were jettisoned onto the front steps, John straightened his clothes and looked at Nancy, who was knotted in a tight embrace with her mother. He cursed himself for ever believing that Nancy was some unholy poison, only important because of the danger she posed to a good Korean boy.

In the Nissan, Nancy and her mother cried with halting gasps as they held each other while John sat ignored in the back, a powerless bit player in their lives.

"I should have helped you back then," John said to Nancy as she covered her face with her sweater. When she did not respond, his voice involuntarily retreated into a whisper, "I loved you."

John sat in silence for several minutes until Nancy's mom turned and said as she wiped her tears, "We are sorry. We will take you home."

"No, no. Please take me back to the hospital," John replied. He was not scheduled for a shift, but he wanted to relieve one of his beleaguered colleagues, as he found himself immune to the fatigue that had saddled him since he began his residency. That night, he wasn't going to work out of any duty he owed to his family or community, but simply because he wanted to heal.

SUE STANDING
Diamond Haiku

Major or minor,
says Baseball Diamond Sutra,
what does it matter?

The boys of summer
know that nirvana is just
one inning away.

Deep in the outfield,
a glove reaches toward sky—
fireflies blink on.

Over the bleachers,
a blank scoreboard announces
no wins, no losses.

SUE STANDING
Orchard House

Far away from this house, far from Concord,
grew orchards where willowy women
read scrolls, not stiff-backed books,
picked pomegranates, not apples.

There, as in fairy tales, houses
glittered like gilt-edged books,
princes and princesses walked in concord
under the sun's golden apple.

But women had to be practical in this house,
while the transcendentalist of Concord,
their impractical father, planned his books
and lectured on the virtues of women:

Cultivate your orchard.
Don't eat flesh or fowl. Stay in concord.
Work and wait. Read the Good Book.
Be high-thinking and plain-living women.

But one of the women
didn't want to be angel of the house—
she wanted, unconquered,
to be her own book.

SUE STANDING
Self-Portrait

I'm a cipher. Before that, I was a loose cannon.
Before that, I was a zealot. I preached on the street corners.
I accosted strangers in subways to tell them I had good news for them.

Before that, I worked on the assembly line in a fireworks factory.
I stuck fuses in firecrackers and poured gunpowder
in the cones of Roman rockets and the spokes of Catherine wheels.

Before that, I made money by selling my plasma
at a blood bank, twice a week.
Before that, I babysat for hemophiliacs.

Before that, I took in ironing. Before that, I polished doorknobs.
Before that, I counted buttons, counted bee-stings, counted my toes.
Before that, I was born—from saint to stain in ten easy lessons.

JANE SUMMER
My Opera Glasses

This audience is dressed
in the old clothes and humiliations
I in my mask, powder woman, sick
of everything, my own
failings most of all. Someone I heard
jumped into the pit
the orchestra, during the third
act and landed between harp
and horn, mangled like a doll
at the bottom of a well. I did that
once, dropped her in the sewer, so
long, said I to her, ta ta, and was done
with the whole business of love.

MARY SZYBIST
Here, There Are Blueberries

When I see the bright clouds, a sky empty of moon and stars,
I wonder what I am, that anyone should note me.

Here there are blueberries, what should I fear?
Here there is bread in thick slices, of whom should I be afraid?

Under the swelling clouds, we spread our blankets.
Here in this meadow, we open our baskets

to unpack blueberries, whole bowls of them,
berries not by the work of our hands, berries not by the work of our
    fingers.

What taste the bright world has, whole fields
without wires, the blackened moss, the clouds

swelling at the edges of the meadow. And for this,
I did nothing, not even wonder.

You must live for something, they say.
People don't live just to keep on living.

But here is the quince tree, a sky bright and empty.
Here there are blueberries, there is no need to note me.

MATTHEW THORBURN
"A Field of Dry Grass"

Osaka

Hard to imagine Bashō
died here in a rented room above a flower shop
in 1694, as I pause today
on Dōtonbori Street, shoppers brushing past
on either side, to gaze
at the giant red mechanical crab
stretching its legs over the door
of the Kani Doraku seafood
restaurant, its eye stalks rotating in a breeze
too high for me to feel. No more
kabuki, no more bunraku.
Now everyone comes here

to eat. Two teenage girls pour
batter thick with ginger and purple
chunks of octopus
into sizzling *takoyaki* griddles
in an open-air café. And up
and down the street I'm distracted again
and again by *ramen, udon,
okonomiyaki, yakitori.* Spiny fish
and green eels swim
in blue-lit tanks. Everything's alive

or just was, is for sale, can be eaten.
"That's not news," the fishmonger
laughs. "Everything depends which end
of the knife you're on."

Once, an old story goes, a monarch—
or perhaps he was a composer?—
lay fading in an upstairs bedroom.
He was so beloved, so missed
and longed-for already
that the townspeople scattered hay
in the cobbled street beneath his windows

to muffle the clanking shoes of horses
passing by. *Falling sick on a journey, my dream
goes wandering,* Bashō's last poem goes,
over a field of dry grass. The thing about
last words, a biographer
said, is being able to get them out

in that last breath
as you squeeze the hand
of a nurse or student crouched
beside the bed. Someone
held his hand, I hope, as someone else
reached for the brush and ink
kept on the table to take down
that poem and save it

for us, whomever we might be.
I like to think the shopkeeper
brought up some flowers to comfort him,
a blur of pink and orange
in a raku vase (a tea bowl, actually,
but the closest thing to hand),
or perhaps a gnarled bonsai
older already than he would ever be.
But no one thought
to write this part down. If I had to

guess, I think he would

have preferred to see once more
the broad green leaves
of the wild ginger that sprang up—
he had looked for the purple
urn-shaped flowers each spring—
along the narrow road
he still followed through his sleep.

ABOUT ALICE HOFFMAN
A Profile by Alexandra Marshall

"When I went to a movie set for the first time, I felt that the person I was most like was the set designer," Alice Hoffman tells me as we sit in a room whose centerpiece is a vivid bouquet of the same tea roses that bloom in the yard beyond the window behind her. "The set designer is building a world that the actors will then walk into, but she's the one who has to create that world. I feel that's what I do as a novelist. It's my job to create the world the characters will enter, and interact in."

We are discussing her newest novel, *The Dovekeepers,* where from scant historical and archaeological evidence about the Jewish exile in the desert following the Roman destruction of Jerusalem, she has created, within that ancient world, a story that resonates as contemporary. "I don't think of myself as a writer of historical novels," she says while acknowledging that she has often set her stories in the past, "but I just had to know what those women knew."

She speaks of the two women who are said to have been the sole adult survivors of the Roman massacre at Masada. Upon her own visit to the site, a powerful experience of the artifacts preserved in the museum led her to read the account written by the historian Josephus.

"When I learned from him that there were two women who escaped with five children—I had never heard that—I decided, well, that's the story I want to tell."

I wonder if in approaching the material she'd asked herself "What If?" What if she'd been in Jerusalem? And she replies, "Not *what if* I'd been in Jerusalem, but *I am* in Jerusalem. I am there! All of these characters are a part of me, but they're working out in their time and place issues that I need to work out in my time and place."

Then what are the questions that she began with? She answers, "I write a novel to find out the questions. In *The Dovekeepers,* I thought my question was how do you survive in a world of war, but I now think my question was something quite different, one I didn't realize until it was over. It has to do with mothers and daughters and the intense relationship between them, and the way people forge those kinds of relationships with those who are not their own biological mothers, and how you learn about life through what you're told by your mother and grandmother and the other women you're close to." To illustrate this conviction, the novel's climactic section called "The Witch of Moab" begins, "My mother taught me everything a woman must know in this world and all it was necessary to carry into the World-to-Come."

Hoffman elaborates, "Growing up in New York and having Jewish grandparents from Russia, the idea of survival was an early fairy tale for me. Finding your way through the woods—finding yourself—is about being able to survive. I'm always writing about survivors—it's my theme—and this has become more my theme now, since I've become a cancer survivor. *The Dovekeepers* starts out with a quote that comes from an ancient spell: 'Let my burden be your burden, and yours be mine.' And I think that's what it's about. There's no way to get through this life without being helped and helping. In writing about war and loss, it really does set you to thinking about what matters, and I think that's what people read fiction for, to think about what matters."

She makes a parallel investment in what matters by giving generously, of her time and energy and money. By donating the advance for a 1999 story collection called *Local Girls,* she initiated The Hoffman Breast Center at the Mount Auburn Hospital, a Harvard University teaching hospital, to consolidate care for breast cancer patients. She has sustained her support with major gifts and by bringing in other prominent writers for annual fundraising events. Modestly crediting her Socialist grandparents for this impulse to provide for others, she also points to the example of Grace Paley, a literary hero "who was always on the front lines" and whom she recruited for a Breast Center benefit. "I give because I've been given so much," Hoffman says, "and because I feel a need to give. I came from having nothing, and I believe that when you can help, you want to help other people."

From her earliest fiction to this most recent work, Hoffman is concerned with the urgent need of women and girls to become independent, as she herself has succeeded in doing. While she was a scholarship student in Stanford University's graduate creative writing program, the legendary editor Theodore Solotaroff published her short story "Property Of" and asked if she had a novel. She promptly wrote *Property Of*, which *Publishers Weekly* called "Highly original…the gang rivalries, the intricate hierarchical subculture of villainous young thugs, and the heady pulse of city life on the run are captured with credibility, even humor." *The New York Times Book Review* celebrated its "Fierce personal intensity," and *The Philadelphia Inquirer* wrote, "Watch Alice Hoffman—there's no denying her power or her talent."

In that first novel (reissued in 2007 as a Farrar, Straus and Giroux Classic in a 30th-anniversary edition), her young protagonist struggles to reconcile intense love with total possession, refusing to become "property" even when her independence is precarious. Working to resolve this conflict marks much of Hoffman's writing, but it is explicit again in a life-and-death sense in *The Dovekeepers*, where the identity of the women—"The Assassin's Daughter," "The Baker's Wife," "The Warrior's Beloved"—derives from the dominant men.

"In the Bible there are little more than a hundred women," she explains. "Not all of them have names, and most of them are talked about in relation to something else, usually a man. *The Dovekeepers* is about having a name, and now that you mention it, that's what *Property Of* is about, a nameless narrator who has no identity, no feeling of self. So, yes, thirty-five years later I'm writing about the same themes."

But as much as her work is about resisting a set of fixed limitations, it's just as consistently about escape, whether from the trap of heroin in her first novel or, here, from an assault by Roman troops that was considered impossible to survive. "Well, until I went there and discovered the Josephus account, I had no idea that anybody *did* escape from Masada," she says of the two women survivors whose story she tells. "And I had no idea when I was doing this book that magic would feature so heavily into it, none at all. Of course I was drawn to it, so I must have had some sense of it, and in the museums, I must have seen magical amulets that I wasn't fully aware of. In my research as a visiting scholar at Brandeis I was shocked at the prevalence of magic in the ancient world, and in the ancient Jewish world. But it was the archaeological artifacts in the museums that brought these people to life. There were the remains of three people who are characters in my book now, and the hair and shoes of a young woman. They came alive for me."

She pauses, as if to allow her freshly cut sun-ripened roses to intervene with their golden-pink oranges and lemony reds, the colors blending the way their perfumes combine. Without changing the subject, she says, "When I went through my treatment for cancer, I read Viktor Frankl's *Man's Search for Meaning*, which was his attempt after his experience in a concentration camp to find a philosophy of why people had to go through brutality and sorrow. What I got from the book was that sorrow defines us and that's who we are, that we would not be able to have the compassion or the faith or the ability to love or the ability to value the world if there wasn't this other component. Evil was created on the same day as good, but why did that happen? The ultimate question we're all asking is why does there have to be evil? Why does there have to be sorrow? Why do people have to suffer the way they do?" But she still concludes, "Even though I write about tragedy, I always think that I'm a much more hopeful individual as a writer than I am as a person. I think to read a book without some hope is really devastating."

In this tension is the balance of opposites that *The New York Times Book Review* celebrated in its review of an early novel, *Fortune's Daughter*, an assessment which can also describe her entire body of work: "It is in its juxtaposition of the mythic, the apocalyptic, with the resolutely ordinary...that this novel finds its unique voice. It is beautifully and matter-of-factly told."

She elaborates, "I have an obsessive desire to write because I was an obsessive reader. I have a need to expand reality, to have it interpreted in some way because, for me personally, it's too painful. In this issue of *Ploughshares,* some of the work is experimental and daring, some is more traditional, and some of it reads like a fairy tale. But every story and every poem was interesting to me, and created a world. There are beautiful poems by a writer I idolize, Ursula K. Le Guin. My favorite book of hers is *The Left Hand of Darkness,* where it's almost as if she's an anthropologist in creating other worlds. I'm interested in unique, singular worlds, and in this issue there are several of them."

I can't resist asking if there's anybody in these pages who reminds her of the young writer she was with her first publication in a prestigious literary magazine—she who is now the acclaimed author of twenty-nine books—and she surprises me by answering, "You never know. Sometimes it's not about how good a story is, it's about how much the person wants to write. There are many great first stories—and it's not that I don't think it has to do with talent, because I do—but continuing success as a writer also has to do with desire. I became a writer in literary magazines, and I think they're so important because it's the way readers get to find out about writers they didn't know about, as well as an invitation to read known writers but with different kinds of material and in a different way. What I was looking for with this issue was what I wanted to read, and that was how I worked as an editor. What do I want to read?"

With her work published in over twenty languages and in more than a hundred foreign editions, when I ask her to talk about her own readers, she says, "I have so many readers who started to read me when they were eleven or twelve, at summer camp. And the interesting thing for me is that I have a lot of mother-daughter readers who say to me there were times when I couldn't talk to my mother or when I hated my daughter or whatever, but we read the same book. I think that's so important because, when you read the same book, you're connecting in some deep way that you may not be able to otherwise. I used to have mothers giving their daughters my books. Now I have daughters doing the same thing."

And does she have mothers and daughters who come together to

Alice Hoffman readings? She smiles, glancing at the vase of vibrant tea roses that she has grown. "I was at a book festival in Tucson when a daughter and her mother walked past my husband, who overheard the girl say 'Oh my God, Alice Hoffman!' and her mother ask 'Who's Alice Hoffman?' and the girl say *'You don't know who Alice Hoffman is?'* So here was this ten-year-old reader introducing her mother to my book, and I feel truly grateful to her. She's my spiritual daughter, that ten-year-old girl in Arizona."

Alexandra Marshall has published five novels and a work of nonfiction. Her first short story, "Child Widow," appeared in Ploughshares *in the Fall 2003 issue, guest-edited by Alice Hoffman, and was named among "100 Other Distinguished Stories of 2003" in* The Best American Short Stories. *She has been a Film Critic for* The American Prospect *and a Guest Columnist for* The Boston Globe, *and her essays, feature stories, and short fiction have appeared in a variety of journals. She was a founder and for many years the director of Emerson's* Ploughshares *International Fiction Writing Seminar held at Kasteel Well, The Netherlands.*

MESSING ABOUT IN BOATS
A Plan B Essay by Michael Anania

There is a moment in every sail, whether you're in a ten-foot dinghy or in a fifty-foot-plus cruiser, when the physics of wind and water catch hold of you. You can feel it in the lift of the boat against your back and in the way the muscles of your legs involuntarily tighten to compensate for it.

In a small boat the tiller pulls at your hand, and the sail, as it fills, takes up the slack in the sheets, lifting the blocks, the single or double pulleys that let you control it, and tugs at your other hand. It is a peculiar and ancient poise, both arms extended, your body stretched backward as the wind freshens. You are part of the boat's ballast, what keeps it upright, so where you sit, how much you lean back, and how you move from one side to the other matter. Just in front of you, sometimes awkwardly so, is a well that holds the boat's dagger board or center board, a flat wooden or metal surface that extends into the water and keeps the force of the wind moving the boat forward rather than let it slide sideways. As your speed increases, water gurgles at the back end of this well and begins to sigh along the boat's sides. Because both boat and sail want to turn, like weather vanes, into the wind, the pressure on the rudder and the pull of the tiller against your hand increase. Let the sail play out and the pressure on the rudder eases. Let it out too far and the sail will lose its shape and flutter, and the boat will stall; so you look up as much as you look ahead, gauging the sail, the long, sweeping line of its trailing edge and the solid palm extended along the mast, the airfoil that pulls the boat forward. With enough speed, as the moving water eddies along its trailing edge, the rudder will begin to hum and the tiller will tremble like a plucked string. This is sailing in its simplest form—a small dinghy, a rowboat really, with a mast, one sail, a dagger board, and a rudder. Every small boat—from windsurfers to complexly tuned racers that can ride across the top of the water—is a variation on this simple design.

Bigger boats, with heavy, fixed keels and displacement hulls, have all the same sensations, though the touch is muted a bit by the effects of size and weight, and their motion is damped in complex arrays of lines and pulleys. Still, the effect of the wind on the sails is the same—the feel of the boat, however heavy, as it lifts under you, the double play of sail and rudder, the hum of the rigging, and the rush of water along the hull. Displacement boats do, however, have their own unique sensations. Their forward speed is limited by the potential speed in open water of the wave their hulls carve out of the sea. The longer the wave, the faster the boat's theoretical hull speed. This limit creates another delight. As the boat approaches its hull speed, it seems to attempt to lift itself out of its own wave. There is a sense of forward surge, which in the best of conditions—good wind and calm water—has an archaic kind of magic, a motion you can easily suppose Odysseus felt as he left Troy, something that binds you to Greek, Phoenician, Egyptian, Viking, and Chinese sailors across time and geography.

There are more dramatic pleasures—the rise and fall of the bow into breaking waves, the strain of the windward rigging, sea froth flying against your face, hail, lightning, the faith you put in your boat's ability to handle the stresses it's subjected to, and a faith, sometimes misplaced, in your own instincts. Running down the face of waves, even a larger boat tends to surf, turning or at least tending to turn its side to the following wave, to broach, and in the worst conditions capsize. Keeping the stern behind you is a matter of concentration and instinct, a feel for the boat that lets you ease, then pull hard against the wheel or the tiller. Your hands grow stiff at it, and your arms ache. Even the best of boats in these conditions can begin what a very experienced sailor friend of mine calls "death rolls," oscillations that seem to exaggerate each other in sequence and feel uncontrollable.

Like gardening, which exists between too little and too much rain, sailing occupies a narrow band of bliss between too little and too much wind, between dead calms and deadly storms. Both its variability and its inherent dangers are part of the appeal. Lake Michigan, where I sail, has all the sudden, violent weather of the Great Plains. Survive a serious storm with nothing worse than a few scrapes and bruises and you've got a story that'll last for years. I read just this afternoon an account of a sailboat going down—not just over but down—in a race for which I have sometimes officiated. I know the skipper, who is a very able racer, and his crew. They spent part of a dark and stormy night clinging to their overturned boat and watched it sink as they were being rescued. Was the boat overwhelmed by the storm that hit it? Did the skipper's instincts fail him? Did the crew's? Was it the wrong boat for the conditions? Back on dry land, one of the crew sent a text to a sailing Web site describing the ordeal, then saying that until the boat went over, it was the best ride of his life.

I started sailing when I was thirteen years old, before I had ever thought of anything as regular and straight as a Plan A, in an eight-foot, square-fronted pram we called a "dink," that sailed backward far easier than it sailed forward. Then I sailed dinghies, scows, and X-boats, all on Carter Lake in Omaha, a muddy, leftover arc of the Missouri River that still marks part of the border between Nebraska and Iowa. I rode my bicycle to the lake in order to sail, sanded and varnished decks and hulls in rented garages through the winter to earn the right to sail in the summer, and one year worked hard, for no pay, for a retired Spanish-American War sailor ("wooden ships and iron men," he said), who had a shade-tree business repairing wooden boats and splicing hemp ropes, just to learn more about boats. I traveled to regattas on Lake Okoboji and Spirit Lake in Iowa and Lake of the Ozarks in Missouri. The desire to sail came from books I read long before I'd ever seen an actual sailboat—*Captain Blood, Young Hornblower,* and Southey's biography of Nelson—and perhaps, as well, from the sheer antinautical nature of Nebraska itself, but the need—I was about to say impulse, but that doesn't quite handle it—has never left me. I've sailed in the Atlantic, off the Bahamas, through the Caribbean, on Lake Erie, and once on the Niagara River, and still live on a sailboat for part of each year. Before I bought my first adult boat, I rented boats by the hour or the day on inland lakes, begged rides from friends, and became the faculty adviser to a university sailing club.

Boat ownership deserves all the jokes made about it. It is costly and frustrating, but it has its own unique pleasures. Every sailboat is a miraculous nest of gadgets—ropes, blocks, winches, pumps, compasses, hand tools, radios, binoculars, knives of all sorts, radar screens, charts, chart plotters, in short, all the dreamt-of toys of boyhood in one small space and the chance, given any little problem or new project, to buy more. "There is NOTHING," the Water Rat says in *The Wind in the Willows*, "—absolutely nothing—half so much worth doing as simply messing about in boats." If you have your own boat, you can "mess about" in it. In the spring you can go to the boat yard, a wonderful maze of keels, rudders, jack stands, and cradles, and hang around with other people who are "messing about in boats," cleaning, sanding, waxing, varnishing, and painting, and facing a long list of seemingly hopeless problems they are always willing to talk about at great length in a vocabulary only other sailors understand. In summer in the harbor, you can mess around some more in a slightly altered but equally loquacious community. You can find company—and advice—by merely changing a bulb in the bow running light. Disassemble something with a lot of small parts, like an outboard motor, and you'll draw a crowd, a mix of well-wishers and disaster lovers. Eventually, you discover an odd contest between "messing about" and actually sailing, a conflict of complementary pleasures. Should you go sailing or mess about? The simple answer, of course, is that you mess about in order to go sailing, but genuine pleasures are never that simple in the demands they make on us.

So my Plan B would have involved living and making a living sailing and "messing about in boats." Doing what? Working in a marina, doing boat deliveries, being a professional skipper on other people's boats, a charter captain, itinerate varnishing, rigging? A recent sailing magazine had a feature on world-cruising hitchhikers, young people, lean and suitably sea-, salt-, and sun-hardened, who sign on as crew on oceangoing yachts just for the ride. A nice thought, full of its own uncertainties, but well out of reach. Plan Bs, often coincident with Fantasy As, thrive on less knowledge than I have of the sailing world. Professional skippers have to cope with nonprofessional owners. Marina work is skilled labor but labor nonetheless. Charter captains have to suffer charterers, and itinerate varnishing is a market cornered by Caribbean geniuses whose brushes don't drip or leave streaks or stray hairs behind. My good fortune is that sailing and all of its delights are still there, however remote any version of Plan B might seem.

Michael Anania's most recent books of poetry are In Natural Light *and* Heat Lines, *both from Asphodel Press. A new collection of poetry,* Continuous Showings, *is due out later this year. His work is widely anthologized and has been translated into German, Italian, Spanish, French, and Czech. His prose fiction has appeared in magazines and in the novel,* The Red Menace *(Avon Books), and a selection of his essays and reviews was published in* In Plain Sight: Obsessions, Morals and Domestic Laughter *(Moyer Bell). A second collection of essays,* Rocks, Paper, Scissors, *will appear in 2012. Anania has been an editor and taught at Northwestern University, the University of Chicago, and the University of Illinois at Chicago. He lives in Austin, Texas, and on Lake Michigan.*

POSTSCRIPTS
Miscellaneous Notes · Winter 2011-12

Zacharis Award *Ploughshares* is pleased to present Christine Sneed with the twenty-first annual John C. Zacharis First Book Award for her short story collection, *Portraits of a Few of the People I've Made Cry* (University of Massachusetts Press, 2010). The $1,500 award, which is named after Emerson College's former president, honors the best debut book by a *Ploughshares* writer, alternating annually between poetry and fiction.

This year's judge was Ladette Randolph, *Ploughshares'* editor-in-chief. In choosing the book, Randolph said: "Sneed's *Portraits of a Few of the People I've Made Cry* is a sophisticated collection. Linked by a common theme of male-female relationships—often sexual, always unbalanced—the stories are mature, beautiful, and devastating testaments to the ways we betray ourselves and each other. No word is out of place, no detail unnecessary. There isn't a story here that isn't a gem."

About Christine Sneed Raised in Green Bay, Wisconsin, and Libertyville, Illinois, Sneed describes herself as a "Midwesterner from birth." Growing up as an only child, she was left alone a fair amount and ended up treasuring her independence—"but I had a lot of cousins, a lot of friends and neighbors," she says, "so I wasn't an only child outcast or anything like that."

Her relationship with words began early: there were always books in the house, she says, and "a lot of respect in my household for literature." Although she filled a few childhood journals with love poems and entries about unrequited crushes, she didn't begin writing seriously until a time-rich year spent studying abroad in Strasbourg during college. "I realized that I could become a writer if I actually sat down and wrote frequently," she says. "I didn't have to ask anyone for permission—I could just do it."

Sneed majored in French and International Business at Georgetown. When asked what she planned to do, she laughs: "I just thought I could get a job—some glamorous job working in a high-rise and wearing nice suits and speaking French, making money, and it didn't happen."

After graduation, she worked for a few years for a company selling highway safety products, and then went on to get an MFA in poetry at the University of Indiana in Bloomington. Post-MFA, Sneed moved to Chicago to work at the Art Institute and began to focus on stories rather than poetry. She still writes the occasional poem, she says, and credits poetry with developing both her attention to language and her sense of writerly playfulness, a quality that she eventually learned could be captured in stories as well.

Over the next several years, Sneed endured streams of rejections and celebrated the occasional success. One of her breakthroughs, the inclusion of "Quality of Life" in *Best American Short Stories 2008*, happened only after the story had been rejected by twenty different journals, before finally being accepted by the *New England Review*.

After several years working at the School of the Art Institute of Chicago, Sneed began teaching at DePaul, where she still works. On a whim, she bundled together some of her published stories with others that seemed to work well with them, and sent the collection to a contest. Allan Gurganus awarded it the Grace Paley Prize. "By turns funny and pitiless," he wrote, "these tales amount to a vision."

Portraits of a Few People I've Made Cry has several elements that lend the collection coherence. All of the stories have an unmarried woman at their center, either single or divorced, and many of them focus on an imbalance in a relationship, often a romantic one—between partners who are rich and poor, young and old, famous and ordinary. With bursts of humor and sometimes great sadness, the stories explore whether the imbalance might be overcome—as in "Twelve + Twelve" or "By the Way"—or if it is more likely to become a poisonous element in the relationship, as in "Quality of Life" or "You're So Different."

Portraits of a Few People I've Made Cry ends with "Walled City," a story that Sneed says has confused some readers. It is a futuristic parable about a city where more and more laws are passed to keep people safe, including banning all conversation. "I really like satire," Sneed says. "It's my natural mode, in a way." Even with the apparent shift in tone, "Walled City" shares a theme with many of the stories in the collection: the human desire to rebel against its own excessive prudence (especially when sex is involved), the question of why, as Sneed says, "people are so willing to do things that they know are bad for them."

A novel called *O Husbands!* is another fruit of this penchant for satire. The book, which Sneed says has proved too weird and possibly too feminist for most editors, tells the story of a female behaviorist who marries three different men. It is an examination of the mores of a society that manages—in the words of Laura Kipnis, one of Sneed's favorite authors—to be "simultaneously hypersexual and to retain its Puritan underpinnings, in precisely equal proportions."

After writing two stories about Hollywood characters in *Portraits*—as well as a later story, "The Prettiest Girls," published in the Winter 2010-11 issue of *Ploughshares*—Sneed recently completed a novel in stories, *Little Known Facts,* about an aging actor (a Harrison Ford type, she says, although not based on him) and his relationships with his grown children. As with some of her earlier work, Sneed tries to explore the problems beneath the surface of an apparently enviable existence, and turn these potentially monumental celebrity characters into real people. "I think we have the license to write about whatever we want," she says, "if we can try to do it authentically."

Little Known Facts will be published by Bloomsbury in Spring 2013. In the meantime, Sneed is full of ideas for more stories and another novel. "I like to know everything I can about people," she says. "So instead of bothering strangers and my friends for private information, I can make all this stuff up. It's really fun."

Emerging Writer's Contest Since 1971, *Ploughshares* has been committed to promoting the work of up-and-coming writers. In the spirit of the magazine's founding mission, the Emerging Writer's Contest honors work by authors who are just beginning to publish and have yet to receive widespread recognition. Next year, we will be presenting Emerging Writer awards for fiction, nonfiction, and poetry.

This year's winner, for fiction, is Thomas Lee for "The Gospel of Blackbird" (see page 123). *Ploughshares* co-founder and contest judge DeWitt Henry writes that the story contains "absolutely sophisticated narration in all regards, with genuine characters, plot, stylistic eloquence, and thematic focus. It has the thickness of a novel. It is also persuasively knowing about both the world of Korean Americans and medicine."

About Thomas Lee Born in South Korea, Lee arrived in America when he was just three years old. After a short time in Queens, he spent most of his childhood and adolescence in Bergen County, New Jersey, in a small and somewhat isolated Korean American community, revolving largely around "one church and one store," he says.

After college at Columbia, Lee went to Yale Law School, and worked at a firm in New York before moving five years ago to Northern California, where he continues to practice. Although Lee has been writing his entire life, he says that it is only in recent years that he has started to view it as more than a hobby, going to workshops at local universities and making time every day to write. Some of his literary heroes include James Baldwin, F. Scott Fitzgerald, and particularly Flannery O'Connor—"not stylistically," he says of O'Connor, "but the theme of divine revelation coming into ordinary lives…that's something I *try* to capture in my writing."

The first draft of "The Gospel of Blackbird" was written about three years ago and began with the line about the shampoo—about how you can cheat on your regular shampoo to make it work better. Years earlier, Lee had seen a Neutrogena commercial on the subject, and hadn't understood what it was talking about (his girlfriend at the time explained it to him). The idea of shampoo infidelity came together in Lee's mind with the details of a friend's romantic troubles, as well as

Lee's own Korean Christian upbringing, and the story began to take shape.

In "The Gospel of Blackbird," as well as some of his other stories, Lee says, he is exploring the idea that Korean Americans are in many ways a "*self*-secluded community." Lee says that many Korean Americans have attempted to separate themselves from mainstream society "in a way that's very self-conscious and very deliberate," and not necessarily in response to hostility or discrimination. Korean nationalism, fostered by centuries of having to resist invaders, as well as the unique Korean vision of Christianity, both strike Lee as playing a role in the community's sense of identity.

In the face of such apparent cohesiveness, Lee is naturally intrigued by people, such as Nancy and John in "The Gospel of Blackbird," who try in both large and small ways to escape the expectations of the culture. "In a world of so many influences," Lee points out, "you're not going to find that you can completely seclude [yourself from] mainstream society," and some of the children are obviously going to "want to break out of that mold."

When asked how his family might react to this story, Lee laughs. "I wonder about this one," he says. "There are themes which I think people will view as very critical of Korean culture, and of Christianity too…but criticism doesn't necessarily mean you're condemning the culture, you're just pointing out issues…All I'm doing is looking at certain individuals from a perspective that I'm familiar with, and saying that this is how they would view Korean culture and the environment they were raised in. And trying to turn that into a story that I hope a lot of readers can relate to."

PEN Emerging Writers Award   David Stuart Maclean, whose essay about losing his memory in India, "The Answer to the Riddle Is Me," was included in the Winter 2009-10 issue edited by Tony Hoagland, has won a PEN Emerging Writers Award. He was nominated for the prize by *Ploughshares* editor-in-chief Ladette Randolph.

GEORGE STARBUCK

From the Archive: "The Work!"
A Conversation with Elizabeth Bishop

Reprinted with newly restored content from Issue 11 of Ploughshares, *Spring 1977 (guest-edited by Jane Shore and DeWitt Henry)*

A gray late afternoon in winter. Elizabeth Bishop, dressed casually in a Harvard jersey, welcomes the interviewer and answers his polite questions about a gorgeous gilt mirror on her living room wall. Yes, it is Venetian, those little blackamoors are Venetian, but it was picked up at an auction in Rio de Janeiro. The interviewer, sure in advance this is nothing to have asked one of his favorite poets to do, squares away with his cassette recorder on the coffee table and pops a prepared question. A wonderful expanse of books fills the wall behind the sofa. Before long there is laughter. A good memory, the thought of a quirk or extravagance in someone she knows and likes, sets Miss Bishop off. The laughter is quick, sharp, deep. No way to transcribe it.

[*Editor's Note:* The original interview was cut and occasionally corrected by Elizabeth Bishop. For this reprint, we have used the original typescript, restoring all of the cuts and keeping the text closer to the recorded conversation. We have, however, left in any content that Bishop added to the typescript to elaborate a story or clarify her meaning, so the version that follows is a hybrid of the two versions. Many thanks to Lloyd Schwartz for telling us about the typescript and sending us a copy, as well as to Frank Bidart, Bishop's executor. The original version of the interview, with all of Bishop's changes, can be found on our Web site, http://pshares.org. Select *Read by Issue* and then navigate to *Spring 1977*.]

George Starbuck: I did some research. I got out the travel book you wrote on commission for Time-Life Books. *There's* geography too.

You tell such wonderful bright clear stories from the history of Brazil.

Elizabeth Bishop: I can't remember too much of that book. At least I choose not to. A lot of it was a catalog. It was edited by Time-Life Books and they changed a lot of it. And I have a lot more *pictures*. There's one—I think the one of Dom Pedro [the last Emperor –ed.] and his official party taken in front of Niagara Falls? Well, there was another pair of those. But that one, I think, is really ironic. He traveled all around this country. And yet he had never been to Iguassu, which is—how much—ten times bigger than Niagara Falls. This was in 1876 and he went to the Philadelphia Centennial. Alexander Bell was there with his telephone—a very young man, whose invention hadn't been used at all. And Dom Pedro ordered telephones for his summer palace, in Petropolis. He also thought that the ladies of his court didn't have much to do, so he took them all back Singer sewing machines—which they didn't like very much. Did you read in that Brazil book how Longfellow gave a dinner party for him in Cambridge?

GS: Yes, and that Dom Pedro was fond of Whittier and translated some of his poems into Portuguese.

EB: So I looked up some of these translations and I thought it would be poems about slavery because Dom Pedro was so very much against slavery. [Slavery existed in Brazil until 1888. –ed.] But they weren't about slavery at all. They were poems about birds, nature poems.

    Poor Whittier was so shy and at the Longfellow dinner party, Dom Pedro, who was over six feet tall, strong and handsome, tried to give the Brazilian *abraço*, twice—and poor Whittier was frightened to death.

GS: You take a set task, like that Time-Life book, and you make it wholly your own. [EB: Not wholly; say two-thirds.] It always seemed that you were just bursting to tell those stories. You're that way with translations. I discovered something. I went into *Geography III* without stopping off at the Table of Contents, and so I went into the Joseph Cornell poem without realizing it was a translation from Octavio Paz.

EB: I think it's a wonderful poem in Spanish.

GS: And in English! That's what I thought: I was reading *your* poem about Cornell. Paul Carroll has a beautiful poem about Cornell's "Medici Slot Machine." And here I'm thinking, Elizabeth Bishop has done an even better poem about Cornell, and I turn the last page and see that it's a translation.

EB: Well, I thought I should put Octavio Paz's name at the beginning, and I tried it that way first. It didn't look right. There was the title, and then the dedication line, and the author's name seemed like too many things under the title, so I decided to put it at the end.

GS: Well, you do good poems about paintings and such. The one in *Geography III* about *noticing* a little painting that has been looked at but not noticed before…

EB: In my very first book I had a poem called "Large Bad Picture," and that picture is by my same great-uncle when he was about fourteen years old. It was a poor family in Nova Scotia, and he went to sea as a cabin boy. He painted three or four big paintings, memories of the far North, Belle Isle, etc. I loved them. They're not very good *paintings*. An aunt in Montreal had one. I *tried* to get her to sell them to me, but she never would. Then Great-Uncle George went to England, and he did become fairly well known as a "traditional" painter. In 1905, I think it was, he went back to Nova Scotia for the summer to visit his sister, my grandmother. He made a lot of sketches, held "art classes" for my aunts and my mother and others. So I have this little sketch ("About the size of an old-style dollar bill"), and that's the one I describe. Helen Vendler has written a very nice paper in which she talks about this newer poem. It hasn't appeared yet.
    Do you use this tape machine to play music, things like that?

GS: This is only the second time I've used it for anything.

EB: I tried doing a lot of letters in Brazil on tape, but I just gave up.

GS: I've even heard of people trying to write on them. Richard Howard trained himself to *translate* using a tape recorder. He was doing De Gaulle's memoirs, all those *nouveaux romans*. Book after book, for a living. He says he disciplined himself to do the whole job in two, or at most three, headlong runs through, reading the French and talking the English into the tape, having a typist transcribe it, running through again.

EB: I didn't know that was the way he did it. What was it, a hundred and twenty-seven novels? I translated *one* fairly long Brazilian book, a young girl's diary. It's probably still full of mistakes, because it was one of the very first things I did. I had just started reading, learning Portuguese. Someone suggested it, and I began. It was *painful*. I can see I had this big notebook, and about a third of the way through I finally caught on to this *child* who was writing. So I began to translate directly on the typewriter, all the rest of it. It took me about three years, as it was. Some people write right off with a typewriter, I think. Dr. Williams did.

GS: Some poets write it out so easily it scares you. We have a neighbor who was a very young nurse working in Boston, at Mass. General Hospital, maybe forty years ago. She told me the story one time, asking me if I'd ever heard of this strange person she worked for. A weird doctor there used to give her poems that he had scribbled on the back of prescription forms, toilet paper, anything, and ask her to type them up. She'd have to go sit on the stool in a small toilet off the hall, the only place she could be out of the way, and with the typewriter on her knees she'd type the things.

EB: Was it—?

GS: Yep, it was Merrill Moore. And he also used to dictate sonnets into a Dictaphone while he was driving. I mean he had a hundred thousand sonnets to get written. Wasn't that the total, finally?

EB: Did she *like* the poems, the sonnets, when she got them?

GS: She didn't know. She didn't presume.

I don't know how you could rush onto tape in translating poems. There's one in which you seem to have discovered something Brazilian that comes out perfectly in early English ballad style. The "Brothers of Souls! Brothers of Souls!" poem.

EB: Oh yes, yes. That "Severino" poem is only a few parts of a very long Christmas play. I saw it given. I've never done very much translation, and I've almost never done any to order, but just every once in a while something seems to go into English. There's *one* poem in there, "Traveling in the Family" [Carlos Drummond de Andrade –ed.], that came out very well, in which the meter is almost exactly the same. Nothing had to be changed. Even *word* order. Of course word order will naturally come out a little bit different, but it just came out *well*. I asked Drummond if I could repeat one word instead of doing it the way he had it, and he said Oh yes, that would be fine. Portuguese has a very different sense of rhythm, more like the French. But every once in a while a poem *goes*.

GS: I'm curious about one of your own that seems to *go* so easily: "The Moose."

EB: I started that, I hate to say how many years ago, probably twenty. I had the beginning, the incident with the moose, it really happened; and the very end; and the poem just sat around.

GS: Did that partial version of it have the other major movement or topic in it: the dreamy conversation, leading you back to the pillow talk of grandparents?

EB: Yes. Yes, I'd always had that. I had noted it, written it down in the diary from that trip. I'm sure it's happened to you, in planes or trains or buses. You know, you're very tired, half-asleep, half-awake. I think probably in this case it was because they were all speaking in Nova Scotian accents, strange but *familiar,* although I couldn't quite make out most of what anyone was saying. But the moose: that happens. A friend wrote me about an encounter like that, with a buck deer. He did exactly the same thing, sniffed the car all over. But in that case, instead of disappearing the way the moose did, he chased the car for about a mile.

GS: You obviously do like to know and use exact geographer's knowledge about things.

EB: Some people don't like that. I've been accused of description. I was reading some new things of Lowell and he said—we've been having this thing for years—he said, "Oh I know, you're going to say I'm *inaccurate.*" The funny thing is that the first poem I read was describing a table his wife had bought, one of those white modern plastic tables I suppose, and he said it was "a dice." And I said: you can't say that. So we spent quite a lot of time getting out a dictionary and looking up things.

GS: You've got the language down pat, and the knowledge of particular things, and let me embarrass you: I admire the philosophy of the poems, the morals.

EB: I didn't know there were any…

GS: OK, OK. But the aubade that ends the book—"Five Flights Up." The way the "ponderousness" of a morning becomes, lightly, our ancient uninnocence: the depression of having a past and the knowledge of what's recurring: "Yesterday brought to today so lightly! / (A yesterday I find almost impossible to lift.)"

EB: People seem to like that poem.

GS: I'm a sucker for that.

EB: I guess it must be an experience that everybody's had. You know, on my first book I got one rather favorable review that wound up saying, "she has no philosophy whatever." People who are city people are often bothered by all this "nature" in my poems.

GS: I suppose Crusoe was a city kid. It's such fun, the accuracy with which you borrow flora and fauna for his little island ["Crusoe in England," in *Geography III*. –ed.]

EB: It's a mixture of several islands.

GS: And the deliberate anachronisms too—like the Wordsworth reference.

EB: Oh *The New Yorker wrote* me about that. They sent the proof back and beside that line was the word *anachronism,* and also some other place in the poem, I think. But I told them it was on purpose. But the blue snail shells, the shells are *true*.

GS: Are there snails like that on—what was his island—Juan Fernandez?

EB: No no no, they're in the Ten Thousand Islands in Florida. Years and years and years ago, I went on a canoe trip around the Keys and a lot of them, but I just remember how fantastic—I think they were tree snails, and I have many of the shells. They were very frail and broke easily, and they were just all over everything.

GS: He's an Adam there and you have this wonderful little penny-ante Eden with "one kind of everything: / one tree snail…one variety of tree…one kind of berry."

EB: The water spouts came from Florida. We used to see them. You know, I *am* inaccurate, though. And I get caught. The poem about being almost seven, in the dentist's office, reading *National Geographic?*

GS: "You are an I, / you are an Elizabeth, / you are one of them." ["In the Waiting Room," in *Geography III*. –ed.]

EB: Yes, yes, that one. Something's funny about that poem and I thought perhaps that no one would ever know. But of course they find out everything. My memory had mixed up two 1918 issues of the

Geographic. Not having seen them since then, I checked it out in the New York Public Library. In the February issue that year, just as I say, there was an article, "The Valley of 10,000 Smokes," about Alaska, that I'd remembered too. But the other things, it turns out, were in the *next* issue, in March. When I sent the poem to *The New Yorker,* I wrote Howard Moss and said I must confess to you that this is a little wrong. They were very nice and said yes we think it will be perfectly all right. But, since then, two people have discovered that it isn't the right issue. They've gone and looked it up! I should have had a footnote.

GS: Well, all the critics are poets and all the poets are critics, but if there's a difference I believe in, it's that, as personalities, critics tend to be more focused on mere literature. And so compendious Richard Ellmann can do that big fat anthology, loaded with *literary* information, but when he has to footnote a place name, he puts the Galapagos Islands in the Caribbean.

EB: He does it to *me.* I say "entering the Narrows of St. John's" and he has a footnote saying *that's* an island in the Caribbean, when it's St. John's, Newfoundland. I use the book in class and practically every footnote is wrong. I finally wrote him a note. He has three or four mistakes just in the few poems I have there. Dates. Just everything.

GS: Maybe he's found a way of having a wonderful collection of letters from all the important poets in America.

EB: Well, he wrote me a very nice letter back. But it was funny. We were reading something in class and I hadn't taken the anthology—I had taken the book itself—one of Robert Lowell's. I was reading from my own copy and two or three students said, "Well, it says right here..." It finally got to be a joke and everything I'd ask they'd read his footnotes in chorus and sometimes they were right and sometimes they were wrong.

GS: Poets *are* really seriously interested in places, in travels, in discoveries about the world...I've been rereading Lowes [*The Road to*

Xanadu, John Livingston Lowes –ed.] and there's nothing at all stupid about that book, but he pretends Coleridge had utterly unaccountable, just out-and-out screwball taste in light reading. *Travel* tales! One of Lowes' tropes is to astonish the reader with what Coleridge got from this obviously frivolous miscellaneous grubbing around in things that nobody in his right mind would read.

EB: Yeah.

GS: It serves his point, but here was an age when *actual* marvels were being discovered. Coleridge went after those books for the best possible reasons.

EB: And how do they *know*? It takes so many thousands of things coming together at the right moment just to make a poem that no one could ever really separate; and say this did this, that did that.

GS: What got the Crusoe poem started?

EB: I don't know. I reread the book and discovered how really awful *Robinson Crusoe* was, which I hadn't realized. I hadn't read it in a long time. And then I was remembering a long-ago visit to Aruba—long before it was a big developed "resort." I took a trip across the island, and it's true that there are small volcanoes all over the place.

GS: I forget the end of *Robinson Crusoe*. Does the poem converge on the book?

EB: No. I've forgotten the facts there, exactly. I reread it all one night. And I had forgotten it was so *moral*. All that Christianity. So I think I wanted to re-see it with all that left out.

GS: When you were very young, which were the poets you started with?

EB: When I went to summer camp when I was twelve, someone gave me an anthology—one of the first Harriet Monroe anthologies.

That made a great impression. I'd never read any of those poets before. I *had* read Emily Dickinson, but an early edition, and I didn't like it much. And my aunt had books like Browning, Mrs. Browning, Thoreau, Tennyson, Ingoldsby's Legends…

GS: But later, when did you begin looking around and say to yourself, "Who, among the poets in the generation ahead of me, are poets I'm going to have to come to terms with?"

EB: That was Auden. All through my college years, Auden was publishing his first books, and me and my friends, quite a few of us, would be very much interested. His first books made a tremendous impression.

GS: I don't see Auden rife in your earlier poems. In fact, it struck me that the closest I had seen you come to an early Auden manner or materials was a recent poem, in the new book: "12 O'Clock News."

EB: That's just recent, all right. I think I tried so hard *not* to write like him then, because *everybody* did.

GS: It's as if, all of a sudden, decades later, there's *On the Frontier*—something you could use in it.

EB: Actually that poem, "12 O'Clock News," was something else that had started years and years before. In a different version. With rhymes, I think. Yeah, I got stuck with it and finally gave up. It had nothing to do with Vietnam or anything when I first wrote it, it was just pure fantasy. This is the way things catch up with you. I have an early poem, a long poem, written a *long* time ago. The second world war was going on, and it's about *that*, more or less. "Roosters." I wrote it in Florida, most of it. Some friends asked me to read it a year or so ago, and I suddenly realized it sounded like a feminist tract, which it wasn't meant to sound like at all to begin with. So you never know how things are going to get changed around for you by the times.

GS: But that makes some sense. Let's see, if I can find it in the book—
Sure:

> where in the blue blur
> their rustling wives admire,
> the roosters brace their cruel feet and glare
>
> with stupid eyes
> while from their beaks there rise
> the uncontrolled, traditional cries.

I'm afraid it's *their* banner now. You'll never get it away from them. By the way, I've heard your "Filling Station" poem used as a feminist tract.

EB: Really?

GS: In a nice apt way, by Mona Van Duyn. She read, at Bread Loaf, in lieu of a lecture, one poem each by about eight American women, with a few words in between the poems. There were a couple of poems which she seemed to want to demonstrate were too tract-y to be of any use. A Robin Morgan poem…

EB: Oh heavens, yes.

GS: In that context, yours did seem a nice wry study of the "woman's touch."

EB: But no *woman* appears in it at all.

GS: But the pot, the flowers, the…

EB: Crocheted doily, yes.

GS: The woman who is "not there," she's certainly an essential subject of the poem.

EB: I never saw the woman, actually. We knew the men there…

GS: But the evidence is…

EB: I never…Isn't that strange? I certainly didn't feel *sorry* for whoever crocheted that thing! *Isn't* that strange?

GS: Well, which *are* your feminist tracts?

EB: I don't think there are any. The first part of "Roosters," now, I suppose. But I hadn't thought of it that way. *Tract* poetry…

GS: What about back in college…

EB: I was in college in the days—it was the Depression, the end of the Depression—when a great many people were communist, or would-be communist. But I'm just naturally perverse—if you want me one way, I go the other way, so I stand up for T. S. Eliot. I never gave feminism much thought, until…

GS: You started to name poets important to you with a man, Auden. Did…

EB: When I was given that anthology when I was twelve or thirteen, in the introduction to it, Harriet Monroe, I suppose it was, talked about Hopkins, and quoted an incomplete fragment of a poem—"tattered-tasseled-tangled." ["The Woodlark" –ed.] She quotes that, and she quotes another two or three lines. I was absolutely *smitten* with those lines, and then when I went to school, in 1927 or 1928, the second Bridges edition of Hopkins came out and a friend gave me that. Well, that was a terrific advantage to me. Marvelous. And I wrote some very bad imitation Hopkins. And tore some of them up.

GS: Did it seem important to notice what women poets were doing?

EB: No, I never thought of it. However, one thing I should make clear.

When I was in college and started publishing, even then, and in the following few years, there *were* women's anthologies. There were special issues of magazines or little get-togethers of women poets and I suppose this *was* the feminist attitude. I didn't think much about it but I just thought that that was a lot of nonsense. And this was from, I suppose, *feminist* principles.

But now, you see, now in these last few years when there's just been this flood of things and I get about sixteen invitations in one year—well I didn't think I could change because I still don't think it's a good idea. I wrote to some of those lady editors and explained. It wasn't that I wasn't all for them and so on, but if I'd had that stand from the very beginning I didn't think I could change. A couple of them reacted rather badly. There was one anthology by Ann Stanford. I must see it. I've seen the table of contents and she found a lot of stuff I've never heard of from the sixteenth, seventeenth, *fifteenth* century. But when I wrote and explained, she was rather cross. I've tried to argue this with Adrienne [Rich] once or twice. I *still* think I'm right. It's one of the few things I think I'm right about.

GS: With Ann Stanford's thing, it was a question of whether you'd let yourself be included?

EB: Yes. I said I couldn't possibly, I never had. And it would be very unfair to others whom I'd already turned down. I told her that hers sounded much better, but even so.

GS: I can imagine a strong feminist argument which says don't be an idealist, be practical.

EB: Adrienne was here and we'd never really argued about it before and there were several other people—old, old friends of mine—and she kept saying "don't you want to be *read?*" and yes I want to be read, but not to that extent.

GS: Well, she convinced me in a related argument one time. I don't think I needed much convincing because I had seen the same thing going on when I was a teacher in a poetry class where there happened to be some good young women poets who were, yes, exploring, systematically trying to find positions for themselves or placements for themselves as women poets. Adrienne said—this is when we were talking about her possibly coming to BU—she said she had gotten to the point where she just didn't want to waste the time, in amenities and dues-paying and awkwardness, that it took, *she* felt, in a mixed class of male and female students...

EB: Really?

GS: Yes. To allow the women, of whom she obviously felt protective, to begin to talk openly and be fully and aggressively participating.

EB: I've never felt this sexual thing in class. Not very often. Once or twice last year with one boy. But they never even talk about it. I don't know but I've never felt it. Maybe I'm blind. Or maybe my classes are more formal.

GS: A novelist at the Radcliffe Institute sat in on Fitzgerald's class. Grace Motjabi. I don't know if you've met her.

EB: No.

GS: She told me how astonished she was—she hasn't taught for a few years, she's been a librarian—at how deferential...

EB: Oh really?

GS: All Fitzgerald's students seemed to be.

EB: Well, maybe mine are. They don't argue much. This year I've had such a good class I can't believe it. I had them here night before last. I've never done that before—and Frank Bidart came, and a few others. They all read some poems. Well, I've never been to other people's workshops, so maybe I should go and see what they're like.

GS: May I try that for you? I don't want one. [A peppermint candy cane, fiendishly sealed in plastic, is in question.] I should carry a pen knife but I don't.

EB: I carry a Swiss Army knife which is defeated most of the time in emergencies.

GS: Do you approve of all the creative writing classes?

EB: No. I shouldn't say this, I suppose. No. I always try to discourage them. I tell students they'd be doing much better if they were all studying Latin. Latin, Greek. They are useful for verse writing.

It's a waste of time. I have a feeling that if there is a great poet at Boston University or Harvard now, he or she is sitting off somewhere writing poetry and not coming to my class or your classes or anybody's classes. Well, I've had some students who have done very well (two or three "geniuses," I think, and several very talented) but that's how many I've had. I think the only thing I hope for is that when they get through college, they'll continue to read poetry for the rest of their lives. What *can* you teach, really teach? I'm a fiend. I assign. I find it awfully hard not to rewrite their things. I try very hard not to say, "This is what should be done," but sometimes I can't resist it.

GS: What happens then?

EB: Well, sometimes they agree with me. Usually they meekly agree with me.

GS: Why does that seem so dangerous and almost forbidden to do? I know it does and I agree with you. But look at painters. I was shocked the first time I went to an art class and saw the professor walking around picking up a brush, a palette knife.

EB: Just changes lines?

GS: Yeah. There was this stuff on the student's easels and he *changed* it.

EB: One boy I had two years ago wanted to write very badly, was very bright, but didn't show too much talent actually. We had some assignments, very strict. When we read some of them out, I was trying to be kind and I said, "Well, after all I don't expect you to do brilliantly on this," and he got furious and said, "You shouldn't say that to us! Any assignment isn't just an assignment, it's a poem!" Well, maybe he's right. Actually in the last two or three years I think they've become more sensible.

I'm thinking about this feminist thing.

I think my friends, my generation, were at women's colleges mostly (and we weren't all writers). You get so used to being put down that very early, if you're intelligent or have any sense of humor, you develop a tough, ironic attitude. You just try to get so you don't even *notice* it.

All my life I've had wonderful reviews. And at the very end they'll say, "The best poetry by a woman in this decade, or year, or month." Well, ha! What's that worth? You know? But you just sort of get used to it. One thing I do notice, though, is that there are undoubtedly going to be more and more good woman poets. I've been reading Virginia Woolf's letters. Have you read them?

GS: No. I've been reading a collection of Marianne Moore letters.

EB: Oh?

GS: Published by the University of Rochester Libraries.

EB: Oh, *I* have that. Anthony Hecht sent it to me. But those aren't such good letters. I mean, of course, they're fascinating. The woman she wrote them to, Hildegarde Watson, who died recently, was probably her best friend. But an awful lot of them have to do with clothes, and chit-chat like that. I have an awful lot of her letters, and some of them, especially the gossipy, personal, literary ones, are wonderful. Telling stories, quoting things, describing. It's very interesting, that little book, but I'm sure she wrote better letters.

GS: And you've been reading Woolf's?

EB: Yes. This is Volume Two. And this is much more interesting. The first volume, I thought, was rather boring, but this is where they [Virginia and Leonard Woolf –ed.] start the Hogarth Press, and it's all about the Press. And you see how *she* ran into prejudice. She doesn't complain about it much, but you sense it. When she wrote *Three Guineas,* her first "feminist" book, she was rather badly treated.

Many times she'll say how unhappy she is about things. Reviews. You know she could be *very* cross. Have you ever read *Three Guineas?* Wonderful little book. I think I have it here. (I need a *librarian.*) This section down here becomes Geography and Travel, and…Oh, here's Woolf. But not *Three Guineas.* I had a friend helping me stow the books. She's very good, but she's made quite a few mistakes. *To the Finland Station* is over here in Geography, lots of little things like that.

I haven't had one of these things for years. [Christmas candy canes on the coffee table.] Peppermint sticks. You know what we used to do with peppermint sticks? You stick it in half a lemon, and you suck it. *Very* good.

I think I've been awfully, oh, asleep all my life. I started out to study music, to be a music major. And somehow I got into trouble with that. I liked it; I gave it up; I wasted a *great* deal of time; I studied Greek for a while; well I wasn't very good at that; then, when I got out of college, I thought I'd study medicine. At that time, I would have had to take an extra year of chemistry and study German. Well I'd *already* given up on German once. I actually applied to Cornell Medical College. But I'd already published a few things, and friends—partly Marianne Moore—discouraged me. Not *just* discouraged me.

GS: Had you submitted things to *The Dial,* or…

EB: *The Dial* had ceased to exist. There were other magazines…

GS: Well, how had Miss Moore found out about you in order to discourage you from going into medicine?

EB: Oh. Well, I knew her. I've written a piece about this that I hope to finish soon ["Efforts of Affection" –ed.]: how I happened to meet her through the librarian in college. I had just read her in magazines and a few pieces in anthologies. The mother of a friend of mine, more educated than my own relatives were, had shown me some things. But in the Vassar Library there wasn't any book.

I asked the librarian why she didn't have a volume of Marianne Moore. She said, "Are you interested in her poetry?" (She spoke so softly you couldn't hear.) And I said, "Yes, very much." And she said, "I've known her since she was a small child. Would you like to meet her?" Imagine! It was the only time in my life that I've ever *risked* meeting someone I admired. The librarian had her *own* copy of *Observations* and lent it to me, but she obviously didn't think much of it, because she'd never ordered a copy for the Vassar Library. There were a lot of clippings—mostly unfavorable reviews. They were all carefully tucked in. And then I went to New York and met Miss Moore, and discovered later that there had been *other* Vassar girls sent down over the years, and that Miss Moore didn't look forward to this a *bit*. But somehow we got along. She met me on the right-hand bench outside the Reading Room at the New York Public Library. Safer than her place to meet people. She could get rid of them quickly. But something worked—a stroke of genius, I guess—because I suggested that two weekends from then I come down to New York and we go to the circus. I didn't know then, but of course that was a passion with her. She went every year at least once. So we went to the circus.

GS: Well, what tone did she take when she found out you were seriously considering giving four years of your life to medicine?

EB: Actually, I didn't tell her I wrote for a long time. Maybe I hadn't even told her then. I guess she must have known by the time I graduated. Even then—I suppose this was a *little* odd even then—we called each other Miss for about three years. But I admired her so *much*.

She had a review of Wallace Stevens that I don't think she ever reprinted. I went over there, to Brooklyn. She waved me through the back door (the elevator wasn't working). And she had two of those baskets for tomatoes, just *filled* with papers. Two bushel baskets. And these were the first drafts of this rather short review. You can see how she worked.

She had a clipboard that she carried around the house to work on a poem while she was washing dishes, dusting, etc.

Now all her papers, or almost all, are in the Berg Museum in Philadelphia. The last few years of her life she sold almost everything, arranged through another college friend. It must have been a life-saver because then she was bed-ridden for about three years. And they have everything there; in fact, they've reconstructed her New York living room and bedroom. At one point they telephoned and they said, "On her desk, remember she had these two figures that were china. Which side was this one on and which side that one? Do you remember which side?" They had made sketches and photographs. So I went down. Looked at it. Painful in a way. But the exhibit of *manuscripts* was marvelous. If ever you want to see examples of hard work, it's just perfect.

She wrote a poem about the famous racehorse, Tom Fool. The man who arranged the collection had done a beautiful job, in glass cases: dozens of little clippings from the newspapers and photographs of the horse. And then the versions of the poem. It goes on and on and on. The *work* she put in!

GS: I'd be fascinated to see how she did those inaudible rhymes—whether that came first or kept changing. How that figured.

EB: She was rather contradictory, you know. Very illogical. She would say, "Oh—rhyme is dowdy." Then other times, when she was translating La Fontaine, she would ask me for a rhyme. If I suggested a rhyme, she would be very pleased. She liked that ballad of mine ["The Burglar of Babylon" –ed.] because it rhymed so well. She admired the rhyme *Many Antennae*. You could never tell what she was going to like or dislike.

GS: That was the other thing about "The Moose." There's that nice casual little six-line stanza, but you establish different interlocking ways of making at least a couple of pairs of rhymes out of the six lines.

EB: I thought it would be regular, but that turned out boring. It seemed almost like a ballad. The first stanza was what I thought of first, and then it just seemed to go. It was so funny, Octavio read it when it was published somewhere. He talks about rhyme a lot. Then he read the first stanza aloud and he said, "Oh, it rhymes! Oh it rhymes some more! Rhymes and rhymes and rhymes!" Robert Lowell is always saying, "I like rhyme." He tries to go back to rhyme but doesn't. Says he can't seem to do it any more. His first poems *violently* rhymed. You—you've written sestinas. Rhymes. I've always thought I'd write a villanelle.

GS: But you *did*…

EB: Finally did. Never do it again.

GS: With that one ["One Art," in *Geography III* –ed.], did you try it first looking for two complete unvaried refrain lines?

EB: No. That was so fast. That was one of those. You know, I have notebooks in which I have started three or four poems repeatedly over the last thirty or forty years and I never can do them. And this one, I just sat down and did, almost "off." I shouldn't say this. But it does happen. At one point I was almost through. There were a couple of lines missing. And Frank Bidart came to call. I said: "Frank! Give me a rhyme for 'went.'" So he *did*. I don't know which line it was, now, but I just put it right in. It was wonderful. Auden has villanelles. "Time can say nothing but I told you so. / If I could tell you I would let you know." And *he* just throws in lines now and then. You can see it. And it works.

You know, it's funny, Anne Sexton had a really wonderful gift for rhyme, which she didn't use very much later on. In a poem which I really don't like exactly, a masturbation poem—do you know that one? The last two or three stanzas are just brilliant.

GS: It's called "The Ballad of the Lonely Masturbator." It happens to be one of the other poems that Mona Van Duyn read in her little "anthology" at Bread Loaf.

EB: Well, the last two or three stanzas are just sheer technical brilliancy.

GS: It was about things like that that she would immediately say, before you could say anything, "Oh, I'm so *clumsy* about form. And rhymes? I don't know how to handle them." It was *truly* the "primitive" part of her art. That is to say, she did it because she really heard it and felt it and owned it. And so she couldn't feel she *understood* it. Then she'd stop and get self-conscious, then she would be try to be more muted or irregular.

But what an extraordinary stroke of good fortune to be a friend of Miss Moore's *before* she knew that you had ambitions…

EB: Oh, I didn't even have ambitions. As I said, I must have been half-asleep. There was an anthology that came out, with ten or twelve young poets—in 1935, I think. Muriel Rukeyser was one of them, I remember. And each of us "young" poets had an elder poet write an introduction. With great timidity I asked Marianne, and she did: she wrote a few paragraphs. And she disapproved very much of some of my language and said so too. It is very funny. I think only one of those poems was in my first book.

The first reading I ever went to, over in Brooklyn, years ago, she read with William Carlos Williams. And she had given *very* few readings. It was in this strange church, in a basement. It was a sort of sloping small auditorium, very steep, and Miss Moore and Dr. Williams were sitting on Victorian Gothic chairs, with red plush backs, on either side of a platform with what looked like a small pulpit at the front. What was so funny—I went over on the subway. I'd never seen a reading before and I was a little late. I had planned to be there *early* but I was a little late. Marianne was reading. I was making my way down the red carpeted steps to the front—there were very few people there—and she looked up, noticed me, nodded politely and said "Good evening!" Then went right on reading. She and Dr. Williams were very nice with each other. I don't remember very much else about it, what they read, oh, *except* that there's a girl, Emily Wallace, in Philadelphia, who is editing Williams' letters, and she sent me a copy a month or so ago of something she had run across: a letter from Williams about this very same evening. And it says, "Marianne Moore had a little girl named Elizabeth Bishop in tow. It seems she writes poetry." Something like that. Of course I never knew Williams.

GS: But you knew Lowell, Jarrell, so many of them…

EB: You know I think we all think this about everybody...every other poet. I didn't know a soul. That is, no one "literary" except Miss Moore at that time.

GS: When did you meet Lowell? I ask this because the way he brought your works into a writing class I visited once at BU some years ago, I had the feeling that he had known you and your work...

EB: Oh, it's been a long time *now,* but for years there, and living in Paris, I didn't know a soul, only Marianne Moore. In 1945 or 1946 I met Randall Jarrell, I can't remember how or where. He came to New York that winter to take Margaret Marshall's place on *The Nation* as book review editor. She left the Jarrells her apartment. I had just published my first book, and Robert Lowell had just published his first book. Randall had known him at Kenyon College. They went to school there together. Randall invited me to dinner. Well, I was scared to death. We got along immediately. I'd read *Lord Weary's Castle,* but that wasn't it. For some reason we just hit it off very well. By chance we'd been to see the same art exhibits that afternoon and we talked about those. Most everybody has this theory that everybody else has a *fascinating* social life...

GS: Did you meet [Reed] Whittemore? He was so active, as an editor, with *Furioso*...

EB: I've never met him.

GS: Did you meet Berryman?

EB: No, I never met him. I went to this awful thing in New York yesterday, hundreds of publishers, milling around together. It made me really aware how I've avoided that sort of thing all my life. I've met more writers in the last three or four years than I had in all the rest of my life put together.

GS: And Brazilian writers?

EB: I didn't meet so many of them. I know a few. The one I admire most of the older generation is Drummond [de Andrade]. I've translated him. I don't know him at all. He's very shy. I was shy. We've met once—on the sidewalk at night. We were at the same big dinner, and he kissed my hand politely.

I do know a few of the younger ones. Vinicius de Moraes, who wrote *Black Orpheus*. He was a very good poet, a serious poet, to begin with. Somewhat Eliot-ish. He gets married regularly. He writes popular songs, very good ones—"Girl from Ipanema," for example, an old one now. He plays the guitar, and has *no* voice at all. Bossa nova. He's a very good poet, and very popular with the young.

GS: Is marrying eight times a rebellion against the old ways of having recognized mistresses?

EB: I don't know. He never has any money. He's a very good friend. He says: "Of course I'm broke. All my wives are such wonderful girls. It's always my fault. And I just leave them everything and take a toothbrush and go." One funny story: I was staying in this place where I had bought an old, old house. It wasn't ready to move into (that took five or six years) and I was staying at a small inn, owned by a Danish woman, an old friend. Vinicius was there too—just the three of us. It was winter, cold and rainy, dreadful weather. We sat, for warmth, in—I don't know what you'd call it—a sort of *cupboard*, a back kitchen for the guests. We just sat there all day, and we were reading detective stories. Once in a while we'd play a game of cards. A terrible stretch. And at night, he'd play his guitar and sing songs. He has some wonderful children's songs. Well, every afternoon a Rio newspaper arrived, one with a gossip column we read avidly. So one afternoon the boy came in with the newspaper and there was a big gossip piece in it about the very same little town we were in, how it had become "fashionable with the intellectuals." And there we were, the only "intellectuals," if that, within hundreds of miles, handing around our Agatha Christies and Rex Stouts and so on.

GS: You seem to write more and more kinds of poems but without exhorting yourself to be suddenly different.

EB: Ha. I know I wish I had written a great deal more. Sometimes I think if I had been born a man I probably would have written more. Dared more, or spent more time at it. I've just wasted so much time.

GS: Would it have been extra works in other genres?

EB: No.

GS: Long poems?

EB: No. One or two long poems I'd like to write, but I doubt that I ever will. Well, not really long. Maybe ten pages. That'd be long. I read Robert Penn Warren's *Collected Poems. He* wasn't lazy. And Cummings.

Oh. I *did* know Cummings. When I lived in the Village, later on, I met him through a friend. He and I had the same maid for two or three years. "Leave a *little* dirt, Blanche," he used to say to her. Blanche finally left them. They wouldn't put traps down for the mice. Mrs. Cummings told her a story about how there was a little mouse that would come out and get right on the bed. They would lie in bed and watch her roll up little balls of wool from the blanket, to make her nest. Well, Blanche was appalled.

GS: Was he sparing the mice on humanitarian, vegetarian principles?

EB: Oh no. Cummings just loved mice. He had several nice poems about mice. He adored them. He used to…
 Well, I haven't said anything profound.

GS: You tell a wonderful story.

EB: Lowell always manages to say something mysterious…

GS: You want to say something mysterious?

EB: !

BOOKSHELF
Recommended Books and Writers

What Is Left the Daughter *by Howard Norman* (Houghton Mifflin Harcourt, 2010): For newcomers to Howard Norman's fiction, this, his sixth novel, will seem deliberately and beguilingly odd. There is, for example, a murder acknowledged from the outset. The first person narrator, Wyatt Hillyer, is writing an account of his life to his estranged daughter, Marlais, who was taken from him as a child by her mother, Tilda, to be raised in Denmark. Now Tilda has died, and Marlais, twenty-one, has returned to Middle Economy, Nova Scotia, the town of her birth, to take the post of librarian. Hillyer lives four hours away in Halifax, and his 243-page letter is an effort to reach out for contact, understanding, and love.

The time of his writing is 1967 (the era of Vietnam, civil rights, and the pill, none of which are mentioned, though the Beatles are) but the era that Wyatt writes about is the wartime 1940s. Wyatt describes his involvement in the murder of a German student, first his rival for Tilda's love, then her husband. Even though Tilda later bears Marlais, Wyatt's child, she never forgives him for this murder, which was committed by her own adopted father, Wyatt's uncle, in an act of crazed hatred for all Germans, with Wyatt helping him to dispose of the body in the sea. One of Norman's ironies is that this provincial hatred of Germans mirrors that of the Nazis toward Jews. As Wyatt later reflects: "My uncle in effect had (to paraphrase Scripture) become what he beheld."

Norman's Nova Scotia is a country of the mind. As in his previous novels, it seems to be a version of pastoral, sheltered from the business of our media-shrunken world. Add to this the historical distance, from the 1920s on, which Norman evokes with a fetish for period detail and a certain nostalgia. This is a world of telegraphs, radios, letters, libraries, phonographs, and museums. There is no TV or mass-marketing, and of course no Internet.

Wyatt's letter begins by recounting the odd tragedy of his parents' separate yet simultaneous suicides when he was seventeen. Following their deaths, Wyatt is taken in by his father's brother and his wife, who earlier adopted Tilda after her own parents died, also simultaneously, from "wasting disease." Living with Tilda under his uncle's roof, Wyatt falls in love. "Completely gone," he writes; "smitten...She was *too much beauty*." But he never declares himself, even when Tilda takes up with the German student, and when both his aunt and his baker friend Cornelia urge him to. "I'm not a student of people," his aunt says, "but when you and Tilda are in the same room, you should just see how you light up." In addition to his uncle's racial hatred, Wyatt's refusal to speak up as a suitor is the second perversity driving the plot. Something in Wyatt holds back, and something in Tilda's curious nature knows of his devotion, but prefers Hans, treating Wyatt as if he were her brother by birth.

Following the murder, Wyatt's uncle goes to prison for life, and Wyatt for three years. Once released, Wyatt returns to East Economy and restarts his uncle's toboggan business at the age of twenty-three. The war is over. Tilda has lost her baby by Hans, and mourns Hans publicly at the docks every morning. Cornelia again tells Wyatt that he loves Tilda and should propose. Tilda is unforgiving, but nevertheless calls him to the library where she is alone and they have sex, conceiving Marlais. Wyatt writes: "Your mother was the love of my life. I was not the love of hers. You became the love of both of ours."

For two years, Tilda, Wyatt, and Marlais live together over Cornelia's bakery, although Wyatt is treated as a pariah by the rest of the town. Cornelia acts as a grandmother, but Wyatt writes that "we didn't add up as a family." Then Hans' parents visit from Denmark and invite Tilda and Marlais to live with them there. Tilda accepts. Wyatt could relocate to be near them, but won't leave the world he knows. Instead, he quits the toboggan business, moves to Halifax, and works as a "detritus gaffer," clearing the harbor of debris. Eighteen years pass in this way. Then he hears from Cornelia: first that Tilda has died and then that Marlais will return to Nova Scotia. At this point, he sits down to write his book-length letter.

While gymnastically artful, and despite moments of beautifully managed pathos (such as the aunt's death), this novel as a whole is not as powerful as Norman's best work. The plot is Dickensian, but the supporting texture is not. Symbolism seems to displace the development of character. What does Tilda's odd penchant for professional mourning and obituaries reveal to us about her? Why her obsession with platitudes? How seriously can we take the uncle's obsession with wartime news and the static in radio broadcasts as motivation for killing Hans? Complexities of psyche remain unexplored, perhaps most importantly in the case of Tilda. This may be because of Wyatt's perspective and tact, but as a central character she remains disappointingly flat, especially compared with more dynamic Norman heroines, such as Imogene in *The Museum Guard*.

The most attractive character is the baker of scones, Cornelia. Baking may have its symbolic aspect—dedication to nourishment—but her humor, humanity, and conscience are fully registered in dialogue and action. She has a teasing, often self-depreciating wit and speaks her mind, for instance calling Wyatt and Tilda's refusal to write each other "the goddamned stupidest, most selfish thing I've heard two people with a daughter doing." She is familiar with grief and manages her own loneliness. She is not odd but is tolerant of oddity. Her love functions as a force to counter fate or fatalism. "Now and then, life can be improved on," she tells Wyatt. Her message, like Norman's, like Shakespeare's in the Romances, is that tragedy can be healed, some lost things found, and that life goes on. —*DeWitt Henry's most recent memoir is* Sweet Dreams: A Family History *(Hidden River). He teaches at Emerson College.*

Unseen Hand *by Adam Zagajewski; translated by Clare Cavanagh* (Farrar, Straus and Giroux, 2011): Adam Zagajewski's newest collection of poems touches on many of the motifs and themes that his poetry is known for. The book is divided into three parts, very carefully arranged, almost like a musical composition. Certain subjects introduced in the first section reappear later in several variations, like Joseph Street in the Krakow Jewish quarter, the river Garonne, and self-portraits. Several of the poems talk about the difficult art of poetry and explore the antinomies of the endeavor.

Zagajewski's voice here is his usual one, quiet and gentle, but the tone of the book is more wistful, somewhat weary, with more silences within and without, punctuated by the poet's intimations of his own mortality. The collection contains strong personal and private notes with many reminiscences of the poet's childhood, his family, and beautiful and moving tributes to his father, who opened his "imagination like a demiurge" ("Now That You've Lost Your Memory"). Mourning the elder man's decline, the poet recalls their hikes in the mountains, his father's reading "To Go to Lvov," the green windbreaker he wore on his trips to Paris, all the moments and details that are the warp and woof of memory.

Some poems here are laments for those who are gone—"candles for my dead"—like "Paintings" for Zbylut Grzywacz, the poet's painter-friend, or "Wall" for Henryk Bereska, a German translator of Polish literature. But the meditations on absence, loss, and all-devouring time are only one facet of the book's tonality. Zagajewski may be aware that "life dwindles" ("The Lovely Garonne"), but his insatiable appetite for "all this great, strange world" hasn't diminished. The book's landscape is concrete, rich, and varied: "strawberry ice-cream melts on the asphalt"; "children play in the sandbox"; "gray sparrows and dapper starlings / still squabble heatedly." The lens scans many different places: Gliwice, Berlin, a Zbigniew Herbert conference in Siena, a train to Warsaw, the Chicago Philharmonic, the Krakow Botanic Garden, Ravenna—not surprisingly, given Zagajewski's geographically complicated biography and extensive travels.

An ardent realist, "slightly sober / and a little touched," the poet observes the world closely, knowing that only the union of an eye and a heart may lead to an immortal moment when one of the world's "zealously kept secrets is revealed" ("Swifts Storming St. Catherine's Church"). This sober and tender observer relentlessly seeks "the flame of rapture / pretty much everywhere, even in the budget theater / the train, and almost every café," since he knows that "the unseen things take flesh" in the quotidian and the ordinary. Talking about his parents' favorite Polish poet, Konstanty Ildefons Galczynski ("K.I.G"), Zagajewski says that trying to salvage "that unseen something / ... may become / the quiet, patient hymn of life."

Unseen Hand is just such a patient hymn. The book's last poem,

"Carts," ends on a powerful note of affirmation: "But that world. / Suitcases packed. / Sing for it, oriole, / dance for it, little fox, / catch it."

The collection is adroitly translated by Clare Cavanagh, and I would have loved for this review to continue on a positive note. Unfortunately, the book exhibits some characteristics of sloppy editing. Either the translator or the editor should have paid more attention to the galleys. One poem in particular shows an egregious oversight. In "Vita Contemplativa," six lines are missing from the middle of the poem; in Polish it has four stanzas, in English only three. The *"pergaminowe twarze"*—"parchment faces" in the Polish original—have been changed to "Pergamon faces," which might seem logical to an English reader since the poem talks about the Pergamon Museum. It's surprising that a publisher as renowned as Farrar, Straus and Giroux could be guilty of such carelessness. —*Ewa Hryniewicz-Yarbrough is a translator and an essayist. Her most recent book of translations is* They Carry a Promise *by Janusz Szuber (Knopf 2009).*

Train Dreams: A Novella *by Denis Johnson* (Farrar, Straus and Giroux, 2011): Denis Johnson's new novella, *Train Dreams*—a brilliantly imagined elegy to the lost wilderness of the early 20th-century Idaho Panhandle and the "hard people of the northwest mountains" who occupied it—focuses on the life story of one such hard person, Robert Grainier.

The novella opens in 1917 as Grainier, part of a railroad bridge-building crew, is swept up in a casual act of racial violence and helps throw a Chinese laborer off the half-built trestle into the Moyea River below. The man escapes death, but Grainier believes himself cursed by him: a curse he considers fulfilled three years later when the fire that incinerates the valley reduces his homestead to ashes and, to all appearances, his wife and young daughter with it.

As a result, Grainer goes from being "a steady man," content with his small family and work on timber and bridge-building crews, to being a loner who resettles on the site of his old cabin. Held to the desolate spot by a ghostly visitation from his dead wife, Gladys, who informs him that their daughter, Kate, has miraculously escaped the fire, Grainier makes a modest living as a hauler, carting goods, corpses, coffins, the injured, and the barely-living both to and from the places that the railroad does not reach.

Throughout his long life, Grainier hears and sometimes witnesses legendary stories in the making. Some are funny, like one about a man shot by his own dog; others are grim, still others magical. Many involve life-and-death ironies, like the story of Arn Peeples, an aging powder monkey who declares that a tree "might treat you as a friend" until you cut into it. Peeples eludes death by dynamite, only to be seriously injured by a falling branch, and then ultimately felled by the flu epidemic.

Though Grainier may be a magnet for stories, he becomes, as one of his cart passengers declares, a "hermit in the woods," no longer used to human touch and speech. His aural landscape is marked by the wail of the Spokane International and the howls of coyotes and wolves. Grainier himself takes up the habit of howling, first to teach one of his dogs how to do it and then "because it did him good."

Grainier's wild howling illuminates one of the book's guiding premises: that those who built the northwest did not just conquer the wilderness but were conquered and absorbed by it in turn. In one significant episode, young Grainier comes across a dying man, a hamstrung robbery victim who seems to be in the process of literally merging with earth: "a mouth hole moving in a stack of leaves and rags and matted brown hair." Even more fateful is Grainier's encounter with a feral wolf girl who haunts the valley: an apparition we chalk up to legend until she appears in the flesh.

If *Train Dreams* imagines a kind of Manifest Destiny in reverse, it remains at heart a gorgeous song of praise for the northwest's chastened white settlers—a song sung in a more subdued but arguably more powerful lyrical voice than fans of *Jesus' Son* will remember. Johnson's love for his subject is palpable in his summation of Grainier as a man who had never seen the ocean, spoken into a telephone, been drunk, or, with the exception of one brief flight at a county fair, ridden on an airplane. The era that could produce such a man is, as the novella's last line proclaims, gone forever. —*Jocelyn Lieu is the author of a collection of stories,* Potential Weapons, *and a memoir,* What Isn't There. *She lives in New York City and teaches in the Creative Writing Program and John W. Draper Interdisciplinary Master's Program at New York University.*

The Foremost Good Fortune: A Memoir *by Susan Conley* (Knopf, 2011): When Susan Conley moves to China with her husband Tony and two little boys, she hopes for adventure, and for her family to grow "in that way you hear Americans do when they head east," but she doesn't know that cancer will play a role in that growth.

Tony is fluent in Mandarin and thriving in his job, but Conley and the boys have a trickier time sorting out where they belong. "Winds of change are sweeping through Beijing," and from the desk in her highrise, Conley can "count a hundred skyscrapers without turning her head," yet down below, an eight-lane freeway snakes around a small *hutong*, an ancient Chinese neighborhood where residents still shuffle to public toilets in pajamas.

Everywhere, the old and the new juxtapose, and the first sections of the memoir are dazzling accounts of a China many of us will never see, taking us beyond the red lacquer doors of the Forbidden City and the span of the Great Wall to places known mainly to residents. With Conley, we join in the search for the perfect dumpling in back alley shops. We hold our breath when stone-faced police request the identification she is not carrying as required. We smile at vast apartment complexes named Palm Springs, Champagne Villas, and Park Avenue, and steer clear of Yummy's, the fast food joint that offers all things chicken: feet, tendons, and heads.

We are also keenly aware of the political. A friend warns that there are four things you can't talk about in China. "The three T's and the One F: Tibet, Taiwan, Tiananmen, and Falun Gong." During Tibetan protests and riots, YouTube fails and televisions tuned to CNN go blank. "It's an odd thing," she writes, "to be so close to the mechanisms of war, but to learn about them only in stolen Internet moments."

Yet we know from the start that Conley will discover she has breast cancer, and artful foreshadowing weaves additional heft through every page. Before the big move, she stopped off in France to teach a long-scheduled writing seminar: "So the boys came to China without me, and I came to China alone, and so far I can't decide if this will be the lasting metaphor for how I experience this country."

On an early adventure to the Chinese countryside, she is reminded of road trips she and Tony took early in their marriage, and how life then "felt like something exciting and vaguely infinite."

She is always conscious of the children, who are funny and honest and provide much of the humor in these pages. "Our move to Beijing has for me become a parenting lesson in how to parcel information: what not to tell, what to tell, and when to tell it." As she panics inside a dark labyrinth at an art gallery, the anxiety becomes something she can't describe. "But what's left is this residue that somehow I'm the odd one out."

Conley reveals herself to us as a watcher, an examiner, someone who deconstructs life's many issues and mulls over her decisions. She is also an accomplished poet, and maintains absolute control of her narrative, resulting in a book that is a structural delight. The whole is divided into small scene-sections, and she goes beyond the use of the present tense to write in a kind of immediate tense:

"Those are my two boys up ahead on the horses."

"Now if I lie very still in my old spool bed, with my left arm propped up on a stack of pillows, I can keep the pain from spreading down my ribs."

"It takes me a minute to realize we're talking seriously about how many years I have left to live."

After a successful surgery and a summer of radiation, the family returns to Beijing, where Conley begins to write the memoir that will help her sort out her relationship to cancer, to China, to her family, and to herself. At first, China feels foreign again, as does her own body. Her own reflections and Tony's Taoist tendencies steady her: "There's one big river we're all swimming in. The trick," he advises, "is to not fight the current. To let the river carry you."

Life can turn on a dime. We all, at some level, know that, and the strong draw of this memoir is its clarity and small truths, conveyed in prose that is elegant and exact. —*Maryanne O'Hara was the Associate Fiction Editor of* Ploughshares *for many years. Her stories have been widely published, and a novel about life during the Depression is forthcoming from Viking Penguin in early 2013.*

How Like Foreign Objects: Poems by *Alexis Orgera* (H_NGM_N BOOKS, 2011): At 113 pages, *How Like Foreign Objects* is an ambitious and meaty first book, filled with poetry that is succinct and captivating. It is easy to be hooked by Orgera's quick wit and deceptively straightforward syntax. Especially, as in "Sleeping with the Dictionary," when she presents lines that offer immediate pleasure while pointing to a deft handling of complex subjects: "I tell you what, it's never the definition / that makes its home in your underwear. // Nine times a man rides up to the house. / Nine times he's turned into a troll // for being obscure." Orgera isn't afraid to be a little enigmatic most of the time, but she is never so challenging as to be uninviting.

How Like Foreign Objects is delightfully hard to categorize. It often seems to be a study in contradictions. Simultaneously funny and somber, direct and obscure, this collection contains many surprises. Orgera is somewhere between Dean Young and Jennifer Knox in temperament and style, combining Young's playfulness with Knox's sardonic irreverence. While not nearly as vulgar as Knox, for which some may find her a bit more palatable, little seems to be above or below Orgera's scrutiny, and even less is so taboo that she would be unwilling to incorporate it. Thus, the navel features prominently in "Retrospective" and a couple's approach to oral sex illuminates the failure of their relationship in "Falling."

Orgera revels in creating spaces where the comic and the sinister intermingle, exposing and emphasizing each other. In "Unlike Many Land Mammals," Orgera even comments on this urge, implicitly acknowledging that, if the strategy occasionally seems debasing, it still cannot be dismissed, for it emerges from a need to take all language seriously: "Until one day you began dying, / you were the bug of my life. To continue / this metaphor would be profane, / but remember that *bug* sounds like *love*." It is precisely this intermingling that makes *How Like Foreign Objects* provocative and charming.

While often funny, Orgera does not rely solely on irony and sarcasm to generate meaning. More often than not, the humor that pervades this work stems from Orgera's capacity, as the title promises, to look at the familiar as though it is foreign. Thus, the book's titular poem—an imagined discussion between an absurdly estranged couple—ends,

"He sees how her questions / are really only the outlines of questions. / How gravity is what solders them glass / to glass to glass like the windows in church."

How Like Foreign Objects is an impressive first book by a promising poet. One hopes that it is only the beginning of a rich and prolific career. Orgera fearlessly heeds Ezra Pound's call to "make it new." As some, including Dana Levin, have pointed out, Pound's imperative has led too many young poets to embrace a façade of originality while failing to generate anything of substance. Orgera's willingness to pursue the new, however, has enabled her to generate poetry that is profound, engaging, and sincere. —*Linwood Rumney's poems and reviews have appeared in* Cold Mountain Review, Cerise Press, *and* Potomac Review, *among other publications. He teaches writing in Boston, where he is completing his first poetry collection.*

EDITORS' SHELF
Book Recommendations from Our Advisory Editors

Tess Gallagher recommends *A Cold Wind from Idaho* by Lawrence Matsuda: "Matsuda's poems break for us all the Japanese American code of silence (*gaman*) toward the indignities of the ten U.S. government-mandated internment camps of WWII, like Minidoka in Idaho where Matsuda was born. He not only educates us in the specifics of the suffering of this time but also brings us into the transgenerational implications of it, connecting this shameful period to both the war in Iraq and the bombing of Hiroshima, where one of his relatives survived near ground zero. The book moves us to new levels of empathy and seeks to heal the speaker, the Japanese American community, Japan in its relation to America, and this nation itself. I admire its dignity, its ferocious honesty, and intimate witnessing of something we thought we knew, but not in this way, until he told us." (Black Lawrence Press, July 2010)

Jane Hirshfield recommends *Invisible Strings* by Jim Moore: "I have loved Jim Moore's brief 'invisible strings' since I first stumbled into a few in a magazine. They are chips of reality, obsidian flakes of the heart and mind. In form they remind me strongly of Mary Barnard's translations of Sappho (the way a set-apart first line functions as both title and opening). Their fragmentary quality, and their deep affirmation of reality as it is, does as well. And, as with Sappho, the worldview here is complex, nuanced, and deep. These poems are also, I should add, thoroughly of our own time, with their references to Abu Ghraib, freeways, and cell phones, and thoroughly the work of an American man of a certain age, looking at his own life and at the lives of others with fully open eyes, mind, and heart." (Graywolf Press, March 2011)

Joyce Peseroff recommends *Kentucky Derby* by Andrea Cohen. "Cohen continues to defy gravity with her wit, while deepening her grounded, hard-won wisdom with poems that hold close and examine the ephemeral, beautiful world." (Salmon Poetry, August 2011)

Jayne Anne Phillips recommends *In Zanesville* by Jo Ann Beard: "for its masterful, completely original take on small town girls and the lives they invent in supposedly sleepy, endlessly complex, Midwest towns." (Little, Brown and Company, April 2011)

Gerald Stern recommends *Bringing the Shovel Down* by Ross Gay: "Realistic; terrifying; tender; beautiful music." (U. of Pittsburgh Press, January 2011)

Gerald Stern also recommends *Pierce the Skin: Selected Poems, 1982-2007* by Henri Cole: "Henri Cole accumulates more and more wisdom, generosity, and loveliness. I was deeply moved by this book." (Farrar, Straus and Giroux, March 2011)

EDITORS' CORNER
New Books by Our Advisory Editors

Alice Hoffman, *The Dovekeepers* (Scribner, October 2011)

Yusef Komunyakaa, *The Chameleon Couch: Poems* (Farrar, Straus and Giroux, March 2011)

Jay Neugeboren, *You Are My Heart and Other Stories* (Two Dollar Radio, May 2011)

Kevin Young and David Lehman, eds., *The Best American Poetry 2011* (Scribner, September 2011)

CONTRIBUTORS' NOTES
Winter 2011

Ruth Blank is currently the Chief Executive Officer of the Sacramento Region Community Foundation. Prior to joining the Foundation, Ruth owned and operated a restaurant and gift shop, and worked in the cable television industry for twenty-five years. Ruth grew up in Philadelphia. She graduated from Sarah Lawrence College and attended the Creative Writing program at Stanford University.

Paula Bohince is the author of two poetry collections, both from Sarabande Books: *Incident at the Edge of Bayonet Woods* (2008) and *The Children* (2012). She has received a fellowship from the NEA and the Amy Lowell Poetry Travelling Scholarship.

Martha Collins is the author of the book-length poem *Blue Front* (Graywolf, 2006), as well as four earlier collections of poems and two co-translated collections of Vietnamese poetry. Two collections of her poems are forthcoming: *White Papers* from Pittsburgh (2012) and *Day Unto Day* from Milkweed (2014).

Kerry James Evans is currently pursuing a PhD in creative writing at Florida State University. His poems have appeared or are forthcoming in the following literary journals: *AGNI, Beloit Poetry Journal, Narrative, New England Review, New Letters, Prairie Schooner,* and elsewhere. His book, *Bangalore,* is forthcoming from Copper Canyon in 2013.

Maia Evrona is a poet and memoirist, as well as a translator. Originally from Massachusetts, she moves around a lot.

James Franco studied literature and creative writing at UCLA with Mona Simpson and Cal Bedient, and has MFAs from Columbia University and Brooklyn College, where he studied with Amy Hempel. His stories have also appeared in *Esquire,* and his collection *Palo Alto* was published by Scribner in 2011. He is now working on his PhD in literature at Yale, and recently wrote and directed a film about the poet Hart Crane called *The Broken Tower*.

Bonnie Friedman is the author of *Writing Past Dark: Envy, Fear, Distraction, and Other Dilemmas in the Writer's Life* (HarperCollins) and *The Thief of Happiness* (Beacon). Her work has been included in *The Best American Movie Writing*, *The Best Writing on Writing*, and *The Best Spiritual Writing*. She teaches at the University of North Texas.

William Giraldi is the author of the novel *Busy Monsters* (W. W. Norton). He teaches at Boston University and is Senior Fiction Editor for *AGNI*.

Jennifer Haigh is the author of four novels: *Faith*, *The Condition*, *Baker Towers*, and *Mrs. Kimble*, all published by Harper. She has won the PEN/Hemingway Award for debut fiction and the PEN/L.L. Winship Award for outstanding book by a New England writer. Her stories have appeared in *The Atlantic*, *Granta*, and elsewhere.

Ann Hood is the author of nine novels, including *Somewhere Off the Coast of Maine*, *The Knitting Circle*, and *The Red Thread*; a memoir, *Comfort: A Journey Through Grief*, a NY Times Editor's Choice and one of Entertainment Weekly's top ten nonfiction books of 2008; and a collection of short stories, *An Ornithologist's Guide to Life*, all published by W. W. Norton.

Joshua Howes recently earned an MFA from Columbia University, where he was a Teaching Fellow; as an undergraduate at Stanford, his fiction won the Bocock-Guerard Prize. He is also a screenwriter and former reporter for the *Chicago Tribune*. Raised in Illinois, he now lives in Manhattan. "Run" is his debut fiction publication.

Rachel Kadish is the author of the novels *From a Sealed Room* (Putnam) and *Tolstoy Lied: A Love Story* (Houghton Mifflin Harcourt), as well as numerous short stories and essays. Her work has been read on NPR and has earned fellowships from the National Endowment for the Arts and the Massachusetts Cultural Council. She teaches in Lesley University's MFA Program in Creative Writing and is a Visiting Scholar at the Brandeis Women's Studies Research Center. She is currently at work on a historical novel titled *Kindness*.

Wally Lamb is the author of four New York Times bestselling novels—*Wishin' and Hopin'* (Harper), *The Hour I First Believed* (Harper), *I Know This Much Is True* (Regan Books), and *She's Come Undone* (Atria). His novel in progress, excerpted here, is tentatively titled *We Are Water*. Lamb also edited *Couldn't Keep It to Myself* and *I'll Fly Away*, two volumes of essays from students in his writing workshop at York Correctional Institution, a women's prison in Connecticut, where he has been a volunteer facilitator for the past twelve years.

Ursula K. Le Guin writes both poetry and prose in various modes, including realistic fiction, science fiction, fantasy, young children's books, books for young adults, screenplays, essays, verbal texts for musicians, and voicetexts. She has published seven books of poetry, twenty-two novels, over a hundred short stories (collected in eleven volumes), four collections of essays, twelve books for children, and four volumes of translation. A collected edition of her poetry is forthcoming in 2012 from Houghton Mifflin Harcourt, as well as a short story retrospective from Small Beer Press.

Sydney Lea has published nine collections of poems, most recently *Young of the Year* (Four Way Books, 2011). His tenth is due in 2013. Winner of the Poets' Prize and a Pulitzer finalist, he founded and for thirteen years edited *New England Review*.

Ann Leary was born in Syracuse, New York, and lived in various towns throughout the northeast and midwestern United States before her family settled in Marblehead, Massachusetts. She attended Bennington College and Emerson College. She is the author of the memoir, *An Innocent, A Broad* (Morrow, 2004) and the novel *Outtakes from a Marriage* (Shaye Areheart, 2008), with another novel forthcoming from St. Martin's.

Thomas Lee is an attorney and writer who lives in Northern California. He is currently writing a short story collection about the experiences of Korean Americans in New York City. His fiction has been published in several literary journals, including the *American Literary Review, Asia Literary Review, Eclectica,* and *AIM Magazine*. His stories have won several awards, including a StorySouth Million Writers Award nomination and recognition as a Finalist in the 2008 Glimmer Train Family Matters Competition. He is a graduate of Columbia University and Yale Law School.

Anna Margolin, considered one of the greatest Yiddish-language poets, was born in 1887 in modern-day Belarus and died in 1952 in New York City.

J. D. McClatchy is the author of six collections of poems, most recently *Mercury Dressing* (Knopf). His book of translations, *Seven Mozart Librettos,* appeared last year from Norton. He teaches at Yale, is editor of *The Yale Review,* and lives in Stonington, Connecticut.

Campbell McGrath is the author of nine books of poetry, most recently *In the Kingdom of the Sea Monkeys* (Ecco Press, 2012). He teaches in the MFA program at Florida International University, in Miami.

Jennifer Militello is the author of *Flinch of Song,* winner of the Tupelo Press First Book Award, and of *Body Thesaurus,* forthcoming from Tupelo Press. Her poems have appeared in

The Kenyon Review, The New Republic, The North American Review, The Paris Review, and Best New Poets 2008.

Joseph Millar's two collections are Overtime and Fortune, both from EWU Press. A third collection, Blue Rust, will appear in fall 2011 from Carnegie-Mellon. He teaches in the low residency MFA at Pacific University and lives in Raleigh, North Carolina.

Marge Piercy's eighteenth volume of poetry, The Hunger Moon: New and Selected Poems, 1980-2010, was recently published by Knopf. She has written seventeen novels, most recently Sex Wars (Harper). Two early novels, Dance the Eagle to Sleep and Vida, are being reissued by PM Press with new introductions. Her memoir, Sleeping with Cats, was published by Harper Perennial. Her work has been translated into nineteen languages.

Nicholas Samaras is from Patmos, Greece (the "Island of the Apocalypse") and, at the time of the Greek junta ("Coup of the Generals"), was brought in exile to be raised further in America, ultimately in Woburn, Massachusetts. He's lived in Greece, England, Wales, Switzerland, Italy, Austria, Germany, Yugoslavia, Jerusalem, and thirteen states in the U.S., and he writes from a place of permanent exile. His first book won The Yale Series of Younger Poets Award; currently, he is completing a new book of poetry and a memoir of his childhood years forced into living underground.

Philip Schultz's most recent poetry collections, both from Houghton Mifflin Harcourt, are The God of Loneliness: Selected and New Poems and Failure, the winner of the 2008 Pulitzer Prize in poetry. His memoir, My Dyslexia, will be published by Norton Press in the fall of 2011. He founded and directs the Writers Studio, a private school for creative writing, with branches in Manhattan, Tucson, San Francisco, and Amsterdam.

Megan Sexton's poems and nonfiction have appeared in Poetry, The Iowa Review, The Literary Review, and other places. She co-edits Five Points and plays drums for the Atlanta-based band, The Skylarks.

Sue Standing is the recipient of grants from the NEA, the Bunting Institute, and the Fulbright Foundation. She teaches creative writing and African literature at Wheaton College (Massachusetts). Her most recent collection of poems is False Horizon (Four Way Books).

Jane Summer, a graduate of Kirkland College, is the author of the novel The Silk Road (Alyson Books). Her poetry and short stories have appeared most recently in Left Curve, The Spoon River Poetry Review, Diner, The Yalobusha Review, and North Dakota Quarterly. She lives in New York City.

Mary Szybist's first collection of poems, *Granted* (Alice James Books), was a finalist for the National Book Critics Circle Award, and her second collection, *Incarnadine,* is forthcoming from Graywolf Press in 2013. She lives in Portland, Oregon, where she teaches at Lewis & Clark College.

Matthew Thorburn is the author of *Subject to Change* (New Issues, 2004) and two forthcoming books of poems, *Every Possible Blue* (CW Books, 2012) and *This Time Tomorrow* (Waywiser, 2013), which includes "'A Field of Dry Grass.'" He lives in New York City, where he works as a marketing manager for an international law firm.

GUEST EDITOR POLICY

Ploughshares is published three times a year: mixed issues of poetry and prose in the spring and winter and a prose issue in the fall, with each guest-edited by a different writer of prominence. Guest editors are invited to solicit up to half of their issues, with the other half selected from unsolicited manuscripts screened for them by staff editors. This guest editor policy is designed to introduce readers to different literary circles and tastes, and to offer a fuller representation of the range and diversity of contemporary letters than would be possible with a single editorship. Yet, at the same time, we expect every issue to reflect our overall standards of literary excellence.

SUBMISSION POLICIES

We welcome unsolicited manuscripts from June 1 to January 15 (postmark dates). All submissions postmarked from January 16 to May 31 will be returned unread. Submit your work at any time during our reading period; if a manuscript is not timely for one issue, it will be considered for another. Our backlog is unpredictable, and staff editors ultimately have the responsibility of determining for which editor a work is most appropriate. We accept submissions online. Please see our Web site (www.pshares.org) for more information and guidelines. Unsolicited work sent directly to a guest editor's home or office will be ignored and discarded. All mailed manuscripts and correspondence regarding submissions should be accompanied by a self-addressed, stamped envelope (s.a.s.e.). No replies will be given by e-mail (exceptions are made for international submissions). Expect three to five months for a decision. We now receive well over a thousand manuscripts a month. Simultaneous submissions are amenable as long as they are indicated as such and we are notified immediately upon acceptance elsewhere. We do not reprint previously published work. Translations are welcome if permission has been granted. We cannot be responsible for delay, loss, or damage. Payment is upon publication: $25/printed page, $50 minimum and $250 maximum per author, with two copies of the issue and a one-year subscription.

BENNINGTON WRITING SEMINARS

MFA in Writing and Literature
Two-Year Low-Residency Program

Read one hundred books. Write one.

Named on the top 3 Low-Residency Programs in the world by *Poets & Writers*.

FICTION ◆ NONFICTION POETRY

Partial Scholarships Available
Bennington College Writing Seminars
One College Drive
Bennington, VT 05201
802-440-4452
www.bennington.edu/MFAWriting

FOUNDER • Liam Rector
DIRECTOR • Sven Birkerts

CORE FACULTY

FICTION
Martha Cooley
David Gates
Amy Hempel
Bret Anthony Johnston
Sheila Kohler
Alice Mattison
Askold Melnyczuk
Brian Morton
Rachel Pastan
Lynne Sharon Schwartz
Paul Yoon

NONFICTION
Sven Birkerts
Susan Cheever
Bernard Cooper
Dinah Lenney
Phillip Lopate
Wyatt Mason

POETRY
April Bernard
Amy Gerstler
Major Jackson
Timothy Liu
Ed Ochester
Mark Wunderlich

WRITERS-IN-RESIDENCE
Lyndall Gordon
Donald Hall
Rick Moody
Bob Shacochis

RECENT FACULTY IN RESIDENCE
André Aciman
Doug Bauer
Frank Bidart
Tom Bissell
Amy Bloom
Lucie Brock-Broido
Wesley Brown
Peter Campion
Henri Cole
Elizabeth Cox
Robert Creeley
Nicholas Delbanco
Mark Doty
Stephen Dunn
Thomas Sayers Ellis
Katie Ford
Lynn Freed
Mary Gaitskill
Vivian Gornick
Barry Hannah
Jane Hirshfield
Jane Kenyon
Michael Krüger
David Lehman
Barry Lopez
Thomas Lynch
Valerie Martin
Jill McCorkle
E. Ethelbert Miller
Sue Miller
Paul Muldoon
George Packer
Carl Phillips
Jayne Anne Phillips
Robert Pinsky
Francine Prose
Lia Purpura
David Shields
Jason Shinder
Tree Swenson
Wells Tower
Rosanna Warren
James Wood

time
3 years

space
Austin

support
$25,000 per year

MFA IN WRITING

THE MICHENER CENTER FOR WRITERS
The University of Texas at Austin

www.utexas.edu/academic/mcw
512-471-1601

SANTA MONICA *Review*
fall 2011
available now

Fictions & Essays

Janice Shapiro / Lisa Richter
Robert Clark Young / Rich Ives / Greg Bills
Haley Carollhach / Michael Cadnum
Lydia Conklin / Sandy Yang / Matthew Crain
Tim Conley / Leyna Krow / Glen David Gold

Cover: Judy Fiskin

$7 copy / **$12** yr. subscription
SM Review / Santa Monica College
1900 Pico Blvd. / Santa Monica, CA 90405
www.smc.edu/sm_review

Boston University
MFA in Creative Writing

BOSTON UNIVERSITY

Our program, one of the oldest, most prestigious, and selective in the country, was recently placed among the top ten by *The Atlantic,* which went on to rank our faculty and our alumni among the top five. The magazine might have been impressed by our two most celebrated workshops—one, in poetry, was led by Robert Lowell, who taught Sylvia Plath, Anne Sexton, and George Starbuck; the other, much more recent, was led by Leslie Epstein, whose students included Ha Jin, Jhumpa Lahiri, and Peter Ho Davies. Our classes still meet in the same small room, which allows through its dusty windows a glimpse of the Charles. These days, the poetry workshops are led by our regular faculty, Robert Pinsky, Louise Glück, and Rosanna Warren—joined this coming year by Dan Chiasson; those in fiction are led by Leslie Epstein, Ha Jin himself, and Sigrid Nunez.

We are also pleased to add that, thanks to a generous donor, we have a new fellowship program that will send a good number of our students for up to three months to do whatever they want, wherever they want—anywhere in the world. And we also manage to provide enough financial aid to cover everyone's tuition and sometimes a bit more.

It is difficult to know how best to measure a student's success or the worth of a program to a writer. Our graduates have won every major award in each of their genres, including, in poetry, the Whiting Award and the Norma Farber First Book Award, along with three winners of the Discovery/The Nation Award and two winners of the National Poetry Series; in fiction, our graduates have won the Pulitzer Prize, the PEN/Faulkner, the PEN/Hemingway, and the National Book Award. Every month one of our graduates brings out a book of poetry or fiction with a major publisher; some, like Sue Miller and Arthur Golden, have spent a good deal of time on bestseller lists. Over the last decade we have placed more than a score of our graduates in tenure-track positions at important universities (in recent years, three of our graduates, Peter Ho Davies, Carl Phillips, and Erin Belieu, have led the creative writing programs at, respectively, Michigan, Washington University in St. Louis, and Florida State).

We make, of course, no such assurances. Our only promise to those who join us is of a fair amount of time in that river-view room, time shared with other writers in a common, most difficult pursuit: the perfection of one's craft. For more information about the program, our visiting writers, financial aid, or our new Global Fellowships, please write to Caroline Woods, Creative Writing Program, Boston University, 236 Bay State Road, Boston, MA 02215 or visit our website at www.bu.edu/writing. **Application deadline is March 1, 2012.**

Boston University is an equal opportunity, affirmative action institution.

THE Rona Jaffe Foundation
WRITERS' AWARDS

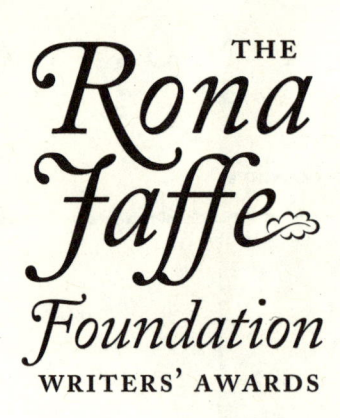

The Rona Jaffe Foundation identifies and supports emerging women writers. Recipients receive awards of $25,000.

2011 WINNERS

Melanie Drane
(poetry)

Namwali Serpell
(fiction)

Apricot Irving
(nonfiction)

Merritt Tierce
(fiction)

Fowzia Karimi
(fiction)

JoAnn Wypijewski
(nonfiction)

WWW.RONAJAFFEFOUNDATION.ORG

MFA
Master of Fine Arts in Creative Writing
fiction ▪ nonfiction ▪ poetry

MA
Master of Arts in Publishing & Writing
book ▪ magazine ▪ electronic

EMERSON COLLEGE
BOSTON MASSACHUSETTS

www.emerson.edu ▪ gradapp@emerson.edu ▪ 617.824.8610

PLOUGHSHARES
Stories and poems for literary aficionados

Known for its compelling fiction and poetry, *Ploughshares* is widely regarded as one of America's most influential literary journals. Each issue is guest-edited by a different writer for a fresh, provocative slant—exploring personal visions, aesthetics, and literary circles—and contributors include both well-known and emerging writers. *Ploughshares* has become a premier proving ground for new talent, showcasing the early works of Sue Miller, Mona Simpson, Robert Pinsky, Tim O'Brien, and countless others. Past guest editors include Richard Ford, Derek Walcott, Tobias Wolff, Kathryn Harrison, and Lorrie Moore. This unique editorial format has made *Ploughshares* a dynamic anthology series—one that has established a tradition of quality and prescience. *Ploughshares* is published in April, August, and December, usually with a prose issue in the fall and mixed issues of poetry and fiction in the spring and winter. Inside each issue, you'll find not only great new stories and poems, but also a profile on the guest editor, book reviews, and miscellaneous notes about *Ploughshares*, its writers, and the literary world. Subscribe today.

Subscribe online at www.pshares.org.

- -

☐ Send me a one-year subscription for $30.
  I save $12 off the cover price (3 issues).

☐ Send me a two-year subscription for $50.
  I save $34 off the cover price (6 issues).

Start with: ☐ Spring ☐ Fall ☐ Winter

Name _____

Address _____

E-mail _____

Mail with check to: Ploughshares · Emerson College
                        120 Boylston St. · Boston, MA 02116

Add $24 per year for international postage ($10 for Canada).